Logic Machines and Diagrams

Logic Machines and Diagrams

Logic Machines and Diagrams

Second Edition

Martin Gardner

With a Foreword by Donald Michie

The University of Chicago Press

The University of Chicago Press, Chicago 60637
The Harvester Press Limited, Brighton, Sussex

89 88 87 86 85 84 83 82   1 2 3 4 5

Library of Congress Cataloging in Publication Data

Gardner, Martin, 1914–
  Logic machines and diagrams.

  Includes index.
  1. Logic machines. 2. Logic diagrams. I. Title.
BC138.G3 1982   160′.28   82-11157
ISBN 0-226-28243-0
ISBN 0-226-28244-9 (pbk.)

for C. G.

Who thinks in a multivalued system all her own.

Contents

Foreword

If the various branches of discovery were to be measured by their relative antiquities, then of all scientific pursuits the mechanization of thought must be the most respectable. The ancient Babylonians had mechanical aids to reckoning, and in Plato's time geometers were already building machines to support formal derivations. The fact, attested by Plutarch, that Plato was himself antagonistic to the development gives a clue to the amazing vitality shown by the logicomechanical study through its long history. Far from sinking into respectability's waveless sea, the arts of logic and its mechanization have been turbulent, intense, schismatic, and now, in the era of the computer, consequential beyond imagining.

The inner energy of these pursuits stems from the pervasiveness of their challenge to prepared positions. From Plato's "thou shalt not" to the "thou canst not" of the vitalists, the mechanizers have been goaded along their chosen trail. Martin Gardner's unforgettable classic of 1958, *Logic Machines and Diagrams,* charted the trail up to that date. It is now reissued in greatly augmented form. Much of the newly incorporated material brings us to the leading edge of today's computer-based work on machine intelligence. It is a pleasure and an honor to respond to his invitation to write this Foreword to the new edition.

Gardner's narrative starts in thirteenth-century Europe, and it starts with a bang. "The *Ars Magna* of Ramon Lull" chronicles the almost unbelievable mechanical devices, doctrines, and strenuous doings of one of the most inspired madmen who ever lived. From here to the new edition's unexpected punch line, we journey through a magical land where it is clarity, not distance, that lends enchantment to the view. No one but Gardner has ever so combined exquisite tracery of detail with the grand panorama. No one else has found his trick of projecting part and whole in one and the same supersharp focus.

Beginning in December 1956, Martin Gardner's monthly series in the *Scientific American* ran for twenty-five years. As inclination moves, he still on occasion returns to the column. A notable "Festschrift" marking the twenty-fifth year was contributed by a group of leaders of the intellectual world. To their praises I must add a word on behalf of those who came to mathematics and logic from the outside. The experience of sitting upon the master's shoulder and gazing through his eyes each month on a new selected scene has bestowed riches upon more journeymen of science than Martin will ever realize.

Over the years the riches have been many times multiplied in his other essays and sustained works. In the turmoil engendered by the first fruits of the computational sciences, some have discerned seeds of social dissolution. Those who see instead a new age of reason in the making owe homage to one of our century's great enlighteners.

Donald Michie
Professor of Machine Intelligence
University of Edinburgh, U.K.

Preface to the Second Edition

When I wrote this book in 1957, the application of Boolean algebra to switching circuits was only beginning to be appreciated, and there was considerable interest in designing special-purpose machines for manipulating elementary modern logic. This interest quickly subsided when the general-purpose computers became smaller, faster, more powerful, and capable of handling formal logics with great ease. As a result, the electrical logic machines described in my eighth chapter became almost as useless to logicians as Napier's bones are to accountants. I have revised Chapter 8 to reflect this change.

Chapter 9, formerly entitled "The Future of Logic Machines," has been completely rewritten as a chapter on artificial intelligence (AI) and its many ingenious computer programs for testing theorems in the first-order predicate calculus and other logics. I have also discussed briefly some work on "heuristic reasoning"—the way people actually think—and on inductive logic machines that try to invent useful scientific hypotheses.

Throughout the rest of the book I have made numerous revisions, mostly in the form of new notes that bring the text up to date or supply information I did not have when I first wrote the book. I regret that I have had neither the space nor the permission to include unpublished material sent to me by readers. In the new Appendix I have made some all-too-brief remarks about the work of three individuals with whom I had correspondence.

xii

I am grateful to Dover Publications for returning rights on their 1968 paperback edition (retitled *Logic Machines, Diagrams and Boolean Algebra*); to the University of Chicago Press for reissuing the book in its present form; and above all to Donald Michie, not only for his generous introduction, but for giving me much needed advice on the rewritten last two chapters.

Martin Gardner

Preface to the First Edition

A logic machine is a device, electrical or mechanical, designed specifically for solving problems in formal logic. A logic diagram is a geometrical method for doing the same thing. The two fields are closely intertwined, and this book is the first attempt in any language to trace their curious, fascinating histories.

Let no reader imagine that logic machines are merely the playthings of engineers who happen to have a recreational interest in symbolic logic. As we move with terrifying speed into an age of automation, the engineers and mathematicians who design our automata constantly encounter problems that are less mathematical in form than logical. It has been discovered, for example, that symbolic logic can be applied fruitfully to the design and simplification of switching circuits. It has been found that electronic calculators often require elaborate logic units to tell them what steps to follow in tackling certain problems. And in the new field of operations research, annoying situations are constantly arising for which techniques of symbolic logic are surprisingly appropriate. The last chapter of this book suggests some of the ways in which logic machines may play essential roles in coping with the staggering complexities of an automated technology.

Although the book consists for the most part of material drawn from widely separated and often relatively inaccessible books and journals, it also contains much that has not previously been published; at least, not in a layman's language. The reader will find, for example, some unfamiliar uses for the well known Venn circles; an explanation of a novel network diagram for solving problems in the propositional calculus; a popular exposition of the new binary method of handling the calculus; and instructions for making quaint cardboard devices that identify valid syllogisms and show the formal fallacies of invalid ones.

The reader may wonder why so much of the first chapter is devoted to the life and personality of Ramon Lull. The answer is that Ramon's life is much more fascinating than his eccentric logic. Other logicians mentioned in the book may have been far from dull to those who knew them, but with the possible exception of Lord Stanhope, recorded details of their lives are comparatively drab and colorless. Lull's Quixotic career is little known outside of Spain and France, and I make no apologies for introducing the reader to one of the most remarkable tragicomic figures of the Middle Ages.

In choosing symbols for the sentence connectives of the propositional calculus I have adopted those employed by Professor Alonzo Church in Volume I of his *Introduction to Mathematical Logic,* 1956. The symbol for negation, $\sim$, I have used throughout, even though the logic under consideration may be the traditional class logic or its modern formalization as Boolean algebra or the algebra of sets. In class logic it is customary to speak of a "complement" rather than a "negation" and to symbolize it as $\tilde{A}$ or A', but in this book so little notation is used for the class logic that it seemed best to avoid introducing special symbols for it.

I would like to thank George W. Patterson and Wolfe Mays for numerous corrections and suggestions; William Burkhart for valuable assistance in preparing the last two chapters; and my wife for all sorts of help in all sorts of ways.

Martin Gardner

1: The Ars Magna of Ramon Lull

Near the city of Palma, on the island of Majorca, largest of the Balearic isles off the eastern coast of Spain, a huge saddle-shaped mountain called Mount Randa rises abruptly from a monotonously level ridge of low hills. It was this desolate mountain that Ramon Lull, Spanish theologian and visionary, climbed in 1274 in search of spiritual refreshment. After many days of fasting and contemplation, so tradition has it, he experienced a divine illumination in which God revealed to him the Great Art by which he might confound infidels and establish with certainty the dogmas of his faith. According to one of many early legends describing this event, the leaves of a small lentiscus bush (a plant still flourishing in the area) became miraculously engraven with letters from the alphabets of many languages. They were the languages in which Lull's Great Art was destined to be taught.

After his illumination, Lull retired to a monastery where he completed his famous *Ars magna,* the first of about forty treatises on the working and application of his eccentric method. It was the earliest attempt in the history of formal logic to employ geometrical diagrams for the purpose of discovering nonmathematical truths, and the first attempt to use a mechanical device—a kind of primitive logic machine—to facilitate the operation of a logic system.

Throughout the remainder of Lull's colorful, quixotic life, and for centuries after his death, his Art was the center of stormy con-

1

troversy. Franciscan leaders (Lull belonged to a lay order of the movement) looked kindly upon his method, but Dominicans tended to regard it as the work of a madman. Gargantua, in a letter to his son Pantagruel (Rabelais, *Gargantua and Pantagruel,* Book II, Chapter 8), advises him to master astronomy "but dismiss astrology and the divinitory art of Lullius as but vanity and imposture." Francis Bacon similarly ridiculed the Art in two passages of almost identical wording, one in *The Advancement of Learning* (Book II), the other in *De augmentis scientiarum,* a revised and expanded version of the former book. The passage in *De augmentis* (Book VI, Chapter 2) reads as follows:

> And yet I must not omit to mention, that some persons, more ostentatious than learned, have laboured about a kind of method not worthy to be called a legitimate method, being rather a method of imposture, which nevertheless would no doubt be very acceptable to certain meddling wits. The object of it is to sprinkle little drops of science about, in such a manner that any sciolist may make some show and ostentation of learning. Such was the Art of Lullius: such the Typocosmy traced out by some; being nothing but a mass and heap of the terms of all arts, to the end that they who are ready with the terms may be thought to understand the arts themselves. Such collections are like a fripper's or broker's shop, that has ends of everything, but nothing of worth.

Swift is thought to have had Lull's Art in mind when he described a machine invented by a professor of Laputa (*Gulliver's Travels,* Part III, Chapter 5). This contrivance was a 20-foot square frame containing hundreds of small cubes linked together by wires. On each face of every cube was written a Laputan word. By turning a crank, the cubes were rotated to produce random combinations of faces. Whenever a few words happened to come together and make sense, they were copied down; then from these broken phrases erudite treatises were composed. In this manner, Swift explained, "the most ignorant person at a reasonable charge, and with a little bodily labour, may write books in philosophy, poetry, politics, law, mathematics, and theology, without the least assistance from genius or study."

On the other hand we find Giordano Bruno, the great Renaissance martyr, speaking of Lull as "omniscient and almost divine," writing fantastically elaborate treatises on the Lullian Art, and teaching it to wealthy noblemen in Venice where it had become a fashionable craze. Later we find young Leibnitz fascinated by

Lull's method. At the age of nineteen he wrote his *Dissertio de arte combinatoria* (Leipzig, 1666), in which he discovers in Lull's work the germ of a universal algebra by which all knowledge, including moral and metaphysical truths, can some day be brought within a single deductive system.[1]* "If controversies were to arise," Leibnitz later declared in an oft-quoted passage, "there would be no more need of disputation between two philosophers than between two accountants. For it would suffice to take their pencils in their hands, to sit down to their slates, and to say to each other (with a friend to witness, if they liked): Let us calculate."

These speculations of Leibnitz's have led many historians to credit Lull with having foreshadowed the development of modern symbolic logic and the empiricist's dream of the "unity of science." Is such credit deserved? Or was Lull's method little more than the fantastic work of a gifted crank, as valueless as the geometric designs of medieval witchcraft? Before explaining and attempting to evaluate Lull's bizarre, now forgotten Art, it will perhaps be of interest to sketch briefly the extraordinary, almost unbelievable career of its inventor.[2]

Ramon Lull was born at Palma, probably in 1232. In his early teens he became a page in the service of King James I of Aragon and soon rose to a position of influence in the court. Although he married young and had two children, his life as a courtier was notoriously dissolute. "The beauty of women, O Lord," he recalled at the age of forty, "has been a plague and tribulation to my eyes, for because of the beauty of women have I been forgetful of Thy great goodness and the beauty of Thy works."

The story of Lull's conversion is the most dramatic of the many picturesque legends about him, and second only to Saint Augustine's as a celebrated example of a conversion following a life of indulgence. It begins with Lull's adulterous passion for a beautiful and pious married woman who failed to respond to his overtures. One day as he was riding a horse down the street he saw the lady enter church for High Mass. Lull galloped into the cathedral after her, only to be tossed out by irate worshippers. Distressed by this scene, the lady resolved to put an end to Lull's campaign. She invited him to her chamber, uncovered the bosom that he had been praising in poems written for her, and revealed a breast partially

* Superscript numbers designate references, to be found at the ends of chapters.

consumed by cancer. "See, Ramon," she exclaimed, "the foulness of this body that has won thy affection! How much better hadst thou done to have set thy love on Jesus Christ, of Whom thou mayest have a prize that is eternal!"

Lull retired in great shame and agitation. Shortly after this incident, while he was in his bedroom composing some amorous lyrics, he was startled by a vision of Christ hanging on the Cross. On four later occasions, so the story goes, he tried to complete the verses, and each time was interrupted by the same vision. After a night of remorse and soul searching, he hurried to morning confession as a penitent, dedicated Christian.

Lull's conversion was followed by a burning desire to win nothing less than the entire Moslem world for Christianity. It was an obsession that dominated the remainder of his life and eventually brought about his violent death. As the first necessary step in this ambitious missionary project, Lull began an intensive study of the Arabic language and theology. He purchased a Moorish slave who lived in his home for nine years, giving him instruction in the language. It is said that one day Lull struck the slave in the face after hearing him blaspheme the name of Christ. Soon thereafter the Moor retaliated by attacking Lull with a knife. Lull succeeded in disarming him and the slave was jailed while Lull pondered the type of punishment he should receive. Expecting to be put to death, the Moor hanged himself with the rope that bound him.

Before this unfortunate incident, Lull had managed to finish writing, probably in Arabic, his first book, the *Book of Contemplation*. It is a massive, dull work of several thousand pages that seeks to prove by "necessary reasons" all the major truths of Christianity. Thomas Aquinas had previously drawn a careful distinction between truths of natural theology that he believed could be established by reason, and truths of revelation that could be known only by faith. Lull found this distinction unnecessary. He believed that all the leading dogmas of Christianity, including the trinity and incarnation, could be demonstrated by irrefutable arguments, although there is evidence that he regarded "faith" as a valuable aid in understanding such proofs.

Lull had not yet discovered his Great Art, but the *Book of Contemplation* reveals his early preoccupation with a number symbolism that was characteristic of many scholars of his time. The work is divided into five books in honor of the five wounds of Christ. Forty subdivisions signify the forty days Christ spent in the wilderness. The 366 chapters are designed to be read one a day, the last chapter to be consulted only in leap years. Each chapter has ten paragraphs (the ten commandments); each paragraph has three parts (the trinity), making a total of thirty parts per chapter (the thirty pieces of silver). Angles, triangles, and circles are occasionally introduced as metaphors. Of special interest to modern logicians is Lull's practice of using letters to stand for certain words and phrases so that arguments can be condensed to almost algebraic form. For example, in Chapter 335 he employs a notation of 22 symbols and one encounters passages such as this:

If in Thy three properties there were no difference . . . the demonstration would give the *D* to the *H* of the *A* with the *F* and the *G* as it does with the *E,* and yet the *K* would not give significance to the *H* of any defect in the *F* or the *G;* but since diversity is shown in the demonstration that the *D* makes of the *E* and the *F* and the *G* with the *I* and the *K,* therefore the *H* has certain scientific knowledge of Thy holy and glorious Trinity.[3]

There are unmistakable hints of paranoid self-esteem in the value Lull places on his own work in the book's final chapter. It will not only prove to infidels that Christianity is the one true faith, he asserts, but it will also give the reader who follows its teaching a stronger body and mind as well as all the moral virtues. Lull expresses the wish that his book be "disseminated throughout the world," and he assures the reader that he has "neither place nor time sufficient to recount all the ways wherein this book is good and great."

These immodest sentiments are characteristic of most eccentrics who become the founders of cults, and it is not surprising to hear similar sentiments echoed by disciples of the Lullian Art in later centuries. The Old Testament was regarded by many Lullists as the work of God the Father, the New Testament, of God the Son, and the writings of Lull, of God the Holy Spirit. An oft-repeated jingle proclaimed that there had been three wise men in the world—Adam, Solomon, and Ramon:

Tres sabios hubo en el mundo,
Adán, Solomón y Raymundo.

Lull's subsequent writings are extraordinarily numerous although many of them are short and there is much repetition of material and rehashing of old arguments. Some early authorities estimated that he wrote several thousand books. Contemporary scholars consider this an exaggeration, but there is good reason to think that more than two hundred of the works attributed to him are his (the alchemical writings that bear his name are known to be spurious). Most of his books are polemical, seeking to establish Christian doctrines by means of "necessary reasons," or to combat Averroism, Judaism, and other infidel doctrines. Some are encyclopedic surveys of knowledge, such as his 1,300-page *Tree of Science* in which he finds himself forced to speak "of things in an abbreviated fashion." Many of his books are in the form of Socratic dialogues. Others are collections of terse aphorisms, such as his *Book of Proverbs,* a collection of some 6,000 of them. Smaller treatises, most of which concern the application of his Great Art, are devoted to almost every subject matter with which his contemporaries were concerned—astronomy, chemistry, physics, medicine, law, psychology, mnemonics, military tactics, grammar, rhetoric, mathematics, zoology, chivalry, ethics, politics.

Very few of these polemical and pseudo-scientific works have been translated from the original Catalan or Latin versions, and even in Spain they are now almost forgotten. It is as a poet and writer of allegorical romances that Lull is chiefly admired today by his countrymen. His Catalan verse, especially a collection of poems on *The Hundred Names of God*, is reported to be of high quality, and his fictional works contain such startling and imaginative conceptions that they have become an imperishable part of early Spanish literature. Chief of these allegorical books is *Blanquerna,* a kind of Catholic *Pilgrim's Progress*.[4] The protagonist, who closely resembles the author, rises through various levels of church organization until he becomes Pope, only to abandon the office, amid much weeping of cardinals, to become a contemplative hermit.

The Book of the Lover and the Beloved, Lull's best known work, is contained within *Blanquerna* as the supposed product of the hermit's pen.[5] More than any other of Lull's works, this book makes use of the phrases of human love as symbols for divine love—a practice as common in the Moslem literature prior to Lull's time as it was later to become common in the writings of Saint Theresa and other Spanish mystics. Amateur analysts who enjoy looking for erotic symbols will find *The Book of the Lover and the Beloved* a fertile field. All of Lull's passionate temperament finds an outlet here in his descriptions of the intimate relationship of the lover (himself) to his Beloved (Christ).

In Lull's other great work of fantasy, *Felix, or the Book of Marvels*, we find him describing profane love in scenes of such repulsive realism that they would shock even an admirer of Henry Miller's fiction. It is difficult not to believe that Lull's postconversion attitude toward sex had much to do with his vigorous defense of the doctrine of the immaculate conception at a time when it was opposed by the Thomists and of course long before it became church dogma.

After Lull's illumination on Mount Randa, his conviction grew steadily that in his Art he had found a powerful weapon for the conversion of the heathen. The failure of the Crusades had cast doubt on the efficacy of the sword. Lull was convinced that rational argument, aided by his method, might well become God's new means of spreading the faith. The remainder of his life was spent in restless wandering and feverish activity of a missionary and evangelical character. He gave up the large estate he had inherited from his father, distributing his possessions to the poor. His wife and children were abandoned, though he set aside funds for their welfare. He made endless pilgrimages, seeking the aid of popes and princes in the founding of schools and monasteries where his Great Art could be taught along with instruction in heathen languages. The teaching of Oriental languages to missionaries was one of Lull's dominant projects and he is justly regarded as the founder of Oriental studies in European education.

The esoteric character of his Art seems to have exerted a strong magic appeal. Schools and disciples grew so rapidly that in Spain the Lullists became as numerous as the Thomists. Lull even taught on several occasions at the great University of Paris—a signal honor for a man holding no academic degree of any kind. There is an amusing story about his attendance, when at the Sorbonne, of a class taught by Duns Scotus, then a young man fresh from triumphs at Oxford. It seems that Scotus became annoyed by the old man in his audience who persisted in making signs of disagreement with what was being said. As a rebuke, Scotus asked him the exceedingly elementary question, "What part of speech is 'Lord'?" Lull immediately replied, "The Lord is no part, but the whole," then proceeded to stand and deliver a loud and lengthy oration on the perfections of God. The story is believable because Lull always behaved as a man possessed by inspired, irrefutable truth.

On three separate occasions Lull made voyages to Africa to clash verbal swords with Saracen theologians and to preach his views in the streets of Moslem cities. On the first two visits he barely escaped with his life. Then at the age of eighty-three, his long beard snow white and his eyes burning with desire for the crown of martyrdom, he set sail once more for the northern shore of Africa. In 1315, on the streets of Bugia, he began expounding in a loud voice the errors of Moslem faith. The Arabs were understandably vexed, having twice ousted this stubborn old man from their country. He was stoned by the angry mob and apparently died on board a Genoese merchant ship to which his bruised body had been carried.[6] A legend relates that before he died he had a vision of the American continent and prophesied that a descendant (i.e., Columbus) of one of the merchants would some day discover the new world.

". . . no Spaniard since," writes Havelock Ellis (in a chapter on Lull in his *The Soul of Spain,* 1908), "has ever summed up in his own person so brilliantly all the qualities that go to the making of Spain. A lover, a soldier, something of a heretic, much of a saint, such has ever been the typical Spaniard." Lull's relics now rest in the chapel of the church of San Francisco, at Palma, where they are venerated as those of a saint, in spite of the fact that Lull has never been canonized.

In turning now to an examination of the Great Art itself,[7] it is impossible, perhaps, to avoid a strong sense of anticlimax. One wishes it were otherwise. It would be pleasant indeed to discover that Lull's method had for centuries been unjustly maligned and that by going directly to the master's own expositions one might come upon something of value that deserves rescue from the oblivion into which it has settled. Medieval scholars themselves sometimes voice such hopes. "We have also excluded the work of Raymond Lull," writes Philotheus Boehner in the introduction to his *Medieval Logic,* 1952, "since we have to confess we are not sufficiently familiar with his peculiar logic to deal with it adequately, though we suspect that it is much better than the usual evaluation by historians would lead us to believe." Is this suspicion justified? Or shall we conclude with Etienne Gilson (*History of Christian Philosophy in the Middle Ages,* 1955) that when we today try to use Lull's tables "we come up against the worst difficulties, and one cannot help wondering whether Lull himself was ever able to use them"?

Essentially, Lull's method was as follows. In every branch of knowledge, he believed, there are a small number of simple basic principles or categories that must be assumed without question. By exhausting all possible combinations of these categories we are able to explore all the knowledge that can be understood by our finite minds. To construct tables of possible combinations we call upon the aid of both diagrams and rotating circles. For example, we can list

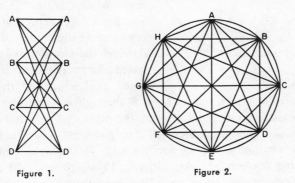

Figure 1.   Figure 2.

two sets of categories in two vertical columns (Figure 1), then exhaust all combinations simply by drawing connecting lines as shown. Or we can arrange a set of terms in a circle (Figure 2), draw connecting lines as indicated, then by reading around the circle we quickly obtain a table of two-term permutations.

A third method, and the one in which Lull took the greatest pride, is to place two or more sets of terms on concentric circles as shown in Figure 3. By rotating the inner circle we easily obtain a table of combinations. If there are many sets of terms that we wish to combine, this mechanical method is much more efficient than the others. In Lull's time these circles were made of parchment or metal and painted vivid colors to distinguish different subdivisions of terms. There is no doubt that the use of such strange, multicolored devices threw an impressive aura of mystery around Lull's teach-

10

ings that greatly intrigued men of little learning, anxious to find a short-cut method of mastering the intricacies of scholasticism. We find a similar appeal today in the "structural differential" invented by Count Alfred Korzybski to illustrate principles of general semantics. Perhaps there is even a touch of the same awe in the reverence

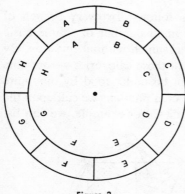

Figure 3.

with which some philosophers view symbolic logic as a tool of philosophical analysis.

Before going into the more complicated aspects of Lull's method, let us give one or two concrete illustrations of how Lull used his circles. The first of his seven basic "figures" is called *A*. The letter *"A,"* representing God, is placed in the center of a circle. Around the circumference, inside sixteen compartments (or "camerae" as Lull called them), we

now place the sixteen letters from *B* through *R* (omitting *J* which had no existence in the Latin of the time). These letters stand for sixteen divine attributes—*B* for goodness (*bonitas*), *C* for greatness (*magnitudo*), *D* for eternity (*eternitas*), and so on. By drawing connecting lines (Figure 4) we obtain 240 two-term permutations of the letters, or 120 different combinations that can be arranged in a neat triangular table as shown below.

BC	BD	BE	BF	BG	BH	BI	BK	BL	BM	BN	BO	BP	BQ	BR
	CD	CE	CF	CG	CH	CI	CK	CL	CM	CN	CO	CP	CQ	CR
		DE	DF	DG	DH	DI	DK	DL	DM	DN	DO	DP	DQ	DR
			EF	EG	EH	EI	EK	EL	EM	EN	EO	EP	EQ	ER
				FG	FH	FI	FK	FL	FM	FN	FO	FP	FQ	FR
					GH	GI	GK	GL	GM	GN	GO	GP	GQ	GR
						HI	HK	HL	HM	HN	HO	HP	HQ	HR
							IK	IL	IM	IN	IO	IP	IQ	IR
								KL	KM	KN	KO	KP	KQ	KR
									LM	LN	LO	LP	LQ	LR
										MN	MO	MP	MQ	MR
											NO	NP	NQ	NR
												OP	OQ	OR
													PQ	PR
														QR

Figures 4 to 9, left to right, top to bottom. (From the *Enciclopedia universal ilustrada*, Barcelona, 1923.)

Each of the above combinations tells us an additional truth about God. Thus we learn that His goodness is great (*BC*) and also eternal (*BD*), or to take reverse forms of the same pairs of letters, His greatness is good (*CB*) and likewise His eternity (*DB*). Reflecting on these combinations will lead us toward the solution of many theological difficulties. For example, we realize that predestination and free will must be combined in some mysterious way beyond our ken; for God is both infinitely wise and infinitely just; therefore He must know every detail of the future, yet at the same time be incapable of withholding from any sinner the privilege of choosing the way of salvation. Lull considered this a demonstration *"per aequiparantium,"* or by means of equivalent relations. Instead of connecting ideas in a cause-and-effect chain, we trace them back to a common origin. Free will and predestination sprout from equally necessary attributes of God, like two twigs growing on branches attached to the trunk of a single tree.

Lull's second figure concerns the soul and is designated by the letter *S*. Four differently colored squares are used to represent four different states of the soul. The blue square, with corners *B, C, D, E,* is a normal, healthy soul. The letters signify memory that remembers (*B*), intellect that knows (*C*), will that loves (*D*), and the union of these three faculties (*E*). The black square (*FGHI*) is the condition that results when the will hates in a normal fashion as, for example, when it hates sin. This faculty is symbolized by the letter *H*. *F* and *G* stand for the same faculties as *B* and *C*, and *I* for the union of *F, G,* and *H*. The red square (*KLMN*) denotes a condition of soul in which the memory forgets (*K*), the mind is ignorant (*L*), and the will hates in an abnormal fashion (*M*). These three degenerate faculties are united in *N*. The green square (*OPQR*) is the square of ambivalence or doubt. *R* is the union of a memory that retains and forgets (*O*), a mind that both knows and is ignorant (*P*), and a will that loves and hates (*Q*). Lull considered this last state the unhealthiest of the four. We now superimpose the four squares (Figure 5) in such a way that their colored corners form a circle of sixteen letters. This arrangement is more ingenious than one might at first suppose. For in addition to the four corner letters *E, I, N, R,* which are unions of the other three corners of their respective squares, we also find that the faculties *O, P,* and *Q* are unions of the three faculties that precede them as we move clockwise around the figure. The circle of sixteen letters can now be rotated within a ring of compartments containing the same faculties to obtain 136 combinations of faculties.

It would be impossible and profitless to describe all of Lull's scores of other figures, but perhaps we can convey some notion of their complexity. His third figure, *T*, concerns relations between things. Five equilateral triangles of five different colors are superimposed to form a circle of fifteen letters, one letter at each vertex of a triangle (Figure 6). As in the previous figure, the letters are in compartments that bear the same color as the polygon for which they mark the vertices. The meanings of the letters are: God, creature, and operation (blue triangle); difference, similarity, contrariety (green); beginning, middle, end (red); majority, equality, minority (yellow); affirmation, negation, and doubt (black). Rotating this circle within a ring bearing the same fifteen basic ideas (broken down into additional elements) gives us 120 combinations, excluding pairs of the same term (*BB, CC,* etc.) We are thus able to explore such topics as the beginning and end of God, differences and similarities of animals, and so on. Lull later found it necessary to add a second figure *T,* formed of five tinted triangles whose vertices stand for such concepts as before, after, superior, inferior, universal, particular, etc. This likewise rotated within a ring to produce 120 combinations. Finally, Lull combined the two sets of concepts to make thirty in all. By placing them on two circles he obtained 465 different combinations.

Lull's fourth figure, which he called *V,* deals with the seven virtues and the seven deadly sins. The fourteen categories are arranged alternately around a circle in red (sinful) and blue (virtuous) compartments (Figure 7). Drawing connecting lines, or rotating the circle within a similarly labeled ring, calls our attention to such questions as when it might be prudent to become angry, when lust is the result of slothfulness, and similar matters. Lull's figure *X* employs eight pairs of traditionally opposed terms, such as being (*esse*) and privation (*privatio*), arranged in alternate blue and green compartments (Figure 8). Figures *Y* and *Z* are undivided circles signifying, respectively, truth and falsehood. Lull used these letters occasionally in connection with other figures to denote the truth or falsehood of certain combinations of terms.

This by no means exhausts Lull's use of rotating wheels. Hardly a science or subject matter escapes his analysis by this method. He even produced a book on how preachers could use his Art to discover new topics for sermons, supplying the reader with 100 sample sermons produced by his spinning wheels! In every case the technique is the same: find the basic elements, then combine them mechanically with themselves or with the elements of other figures. Dozens of his books deal with applications of the Art, introducing endless small variations of terminology and symbols. Some of these works are introductions to more comprehensive treatises. Some are brief, popular versions for less intellectual readers who find it hard to comprehend the more involved figures. For example, the categories of certain basic figures are reduced from sixteen to nine (see Figure 9). These simpler ninefold circles are the ones encountered in the writings of Bruno, Kircher, and other Renaissance Lullists, in Hegel's description of the Art (*Lectures on the History of Philosophy,* Vol. 3), and in most modern histories of thought that find space for Lull's method. Two of Lull's treatises on his Art are written entirely in Catalan verse.

One of Lull's ninefold circles is concerned with objects of knowledge—God, angel, heaven, man, the imagination, the sensitive, the negative, the elementary, and the instrumental. Another asks the nine questions—whether? what? whence? why? how great? of what kind? when? where? and how? Many of Lull's books devote considerable space to questions suggested by these and similar circles. *The Book of the Ascent and Descent of the Intellect,* using a twelvefold and a fivefold circle in application to eight categories (stone, flame, plant, animal, man, heaven, angel, God) considers such scientific posers as: Where does the flame go when a candle is put out? Why does rue strengthen the eyes and onions weaken them? Where does the cold go when a stone is warmed?

In another interesting work Lull uses his Art to explain to a hermit the meaning of some of the *Sentences* of Peter Lombard. The book takes up such typical medieval problems as: Could Adam and Eve have cohabited before they ate their first food? If a child is slain in the womb of a martyred mother, will it be saved by a baptism of blood? How do angels speak to each other? How do angels pass from one place to another in an instant of time? Can God make matter without form? Can He damn Peter and save Judas? Can a fallen angel repent? In one book, the *Tree of Science,* over four thousand such questions are raised! Sometimes Lull gives the combination of terms in which the answer may be found, together with a fully reasoned commentary. Sometimes he merely indicates the figures to be used, letting the reader find the right combinations for himself. At other times he leaves the question entirely unanswered.

The number of concentric circles to be used in the same figure varies from time to time—two or three being the most common. The method reaches its climax in a varicolored metal device called the *figura universalis* which has no less than fourteen concentric circles! The mind reels at the number and complexity of topics that can be explored by this fantastic instrument.

Before passing on to an evaluation of Lull's method, it should be mentioned that he also frequently employed the diagrammatic device of the tree to indicate subdivisions of genera and species. For Lull it was both an illustrative and a mnemonic device. His *Principles of Medicine,* for example, pictures his subject matter as a tree with four roots (the four humors) and two trunks (ancient and modern medicine). The trunks branch off into various boughs on which flowers bloom, each flower having a symbolic meaning (air, exercise, food, sleep, etc.). Colored triangles, squares, and other Lullian figures also are attached to the branches.

None of Lull's scientific writings, least of all his medical works, added to the scientific knowledge of his time. In such respects he was neither ahead nor behind his contemporaries. Alchemy and geomancy he rejected as worthless. Necromancy, or the art of communicating with the dead, he accepted in a sense common in his day and still surviving in the attitude of many orthodox churchmen; miraculous results are not denied, but they are regarded as demonic in origin. Lull even used the success of necromancers as a kind of proof of the existence of God. The fallen angels could not exist, he argued, if God had not created them.

There is no doubt about Lull's complete acceptance of astrology. His so-called astronomical writings actually are astrological, showing how his circles can be used to reveal various favorable and unfavorable combinations of planets within the signs of the zodiac. In one of his books he applies astrology to medicine. By means of the Art he obtains sixteen combinations of the four elements (earth, air, fire, water) and the four properties (hot, cold, moist, dry).

These are then combined in various ways with the signs of the zodiac to answer medical questions concerning diet, evacuation, preparation of medicines, fevers, color of urine, and so on.

There is no indication that Ramon Lull, the Doctor Illuminatus as he was later called, ever seriously doubted that his Art was the product of divine illumination. But one remarkable poem, the *Desconort* ("Disconsolateness"), suggests that at times he may have been tormented by the thought that possibly his Art was worthless. The poem is ingeniously constructed of sixty-nine stanzas, each consisting of twelve lines that end in the same rhyme. It opens with Lull's bitter reflections on his failure for the past thirty years to achieve any of his missionary projects. Seeking consolation in the woods, he comes upon the inevitable hermit and pours out to him the nature of his sorrows. He is a lonely, neglected man. People laugh at him and call him a fool. His great Art is ridiculed and ignored. Instead of sympathizing, the hermit tries to prove to Ramon that he deserves this ridicule. If his books on the Art are read by men "as fast as a cat that runs through burning coals," perhaps this is because the dogmas of the church cannot be demonstrated by reason. If they could be, then what merit would there be in believing them? In addition, the hermit argues, if Lull's method is so valuable, how is it that the ancient philosophers never thought of it? And if it truly comes from God, what reason has he to fear it will ever be lost?

Lull replies so eloquently to these objections that we soon find the hermit begging forgiveness for all he has said, offering to join Ramon in his labors, and even weeping because he had not learned the Art earlier in life!

Perhaps the most striking illustration of how greatly Lull valued his method is the legend of how he happened to join the third order of Franciscans. He had made all necessary arrangements for his first missionary trip to North Africa, but at the last moment, tormented by doubts and fears of imprisonment and death, he allowed the boat to sail without him. This precipitated a mental breakdown that threw him into a state of profound depression. He was carried into a Dominican church and while praying there he saw a light like a star and heard a voice speak from above: "Within this order thou shalt be saved." Lull hesitated to join the order because he knew the Dominicans had little interest in his Art whereas the

Franciscans had found it of value. A second time the voice spoke from the light, this time threateningly: "And did I not tell thee that only in the order of the Preachers thou wouldst find salvation?" Lull finally decided it would be better to undergo personal damnation than risk the loss of his Art whereby others might be saved. Ignoring the vision, he joined the Franciscans.

It is clear from Lull's writings that he thought of his method as possessing many values. The diagrams and circles aid the understanding by making it easy to visualize the elements of a given argument. They have considerable mnemonic value, an aspect of his Art that appealed strongly to Lull's Renaissance admirers. They have rhetorical value, not only arousing interest by their picturesque, cabalistic character, but also aiding in the demonstration of proofs and the teaching of doctrines. It is an investigative and inventive art. When ideas are combined in all possible ways, the new combinations start the mind thinking along novel channels and one is led to discover fresh truths and arguments, or to make new inventions. Finally, the Art possesses a kind of deductive power.

Lull did not, however, regard his method as a substitute for the formal logic of Aristotle and the schoolmen. He was thoroughly familiar with traditional logic and his writings even include the popular medieval diagrams of immediate inference and the various syllogistic figures and moods. He certainly did not think that the mere juxtaposition of terms provided in themselves a proof by "necessary reasons." He did think, however, that by the mechanical combination of terms one could discover the necessary building blocks out of which valid arguments could then be constructed. Like his colleagues among the schoolmen, he was convinced that each branch of knowledge rested on a relatively few, self-evident principles which formed the structure of all knowledge in the same way that geometrical theorems were formed out of basic axioms. It was natural for him to suppose that by exhausting the combinations of such principles one might thereby explore all possible structures of truth and so obtain universal knowledge.

There is a sense, of course, in which Lull's method of exploration does possess a formal deductive character. If we wish to exhaust the possible combinations of given sets of terms, then Lull's method obviously will do this for us in an irrefutable way. Considered mathematically, the technique is sound, though even in its day it was essentially trivial. Tabulating combinations of terms was certainly a familiar process to mathematicians as far back as the Greeks, and it would be surprising indeed if no one before Lull had thought of using movable circles as a device for obtaining such tables. Lull's mistake, in large part a product of the philosophic temper of his age, was to suppose that his combinatorial method had useful application to subject matters where today we see clearly that it does not apply. Not only is there a distressing lack of "analytic" structure in areas of knowledge outside of logic and mathematics, there is not even agreement on what to regard as the most primitive, "self-evident" principles in any given subject matter. Lull naturally chose for his categories those that were implicit in the dogmas and opinions he wished to establish. The result, as Chesterton might have said, was that Lull's circles led him in most cases into proofs that were circular. Other schoolmen were of course often guilty of question begging, but it was Lull's peculiar distinction to base this type of reasoning on such an artificial, mechanical technique that it amounted virtually to a satire of scholasticism, a sort of hilarious caricature of medieval argumentation.

We have mentioned earlier that it was Leibnitz who first saw in Lull's method the possibility of applying it to formal logic.[8] For example, in his *Dissertio de arte combinatoria* Leibnitz constructs an exhaustive table of all possible combinations of premises and conclusions in the traditional syllogism. The false syllogisms are then eliminated, leaving no doubt as to the number of valid ones, though of course revealing nothing that was not perfectly familiar to Aristotle. A somewhat similar technique of elimination was used by Jevons (as we shall see in Chapter 5) in his "logical alphabet" and his logic machine, and is used today in the construction of matrix tables for problems in symbolic logic. Like Lull, however, Leibnitz failed to see how restricted was the application of such a technique, and his vision of reducing all knowledge to composite terms built up out of simple elements and capable of being manipulated like mathematical symbols is certainly as wildly visionary as Lull's similar dream. It is only in the dimmest sense that Leibnitz can be said to anticipate modern symbolic logic. In Lull's case the anticipation is so remote that it scarcely deserves mention.

Still, there is something to be said for certain limited applications of Lull's circles, though it must be confessed that the applications are to subject matters which Lull would have considered frivolous. For example, parents seeking a first and middle name for a newborn baby might find it useful to write all acceptable first names in one circle and acceptable middle names on a larger circle, then rotate the inner circle to explore the possible combinations. Ancient coding and decoding devices for secret ciphers make use of Lullian-type wheels. Artists and decorators sometimes employ color wheels for exploring color combinations. Anagram puzzles often can be solved quickly by using Lullian circles to permute the required letters. A cardboard toy for children consists of a rotating circle with animal pictures around the circumference, half of each animal on the circle and half on the sheet to which the wheel is fastened. Turning the circle produces amusing combinations—a giraffe's head on the body of a hippopotamus, and so on. One thinks also of Sam Loyd's famous "Get off the earth" paradox. Renan once described Lull's circles as "magic," but in turning Loyd's wheel the picture of an entire Chinese warrior is made to vanish before your very eyes.[9] It is amusing to imagine how Lull would have analyzed Loyd's paradox, for his aptitude for mathematical thinking was not very high.

Even closer to the spirit of Lull's method is a device that was sold to fiction writers many years ago and titled, if I remember correctly, the "Plot Genii." By turning concentric circles one could obtain different combinations of plot elements. (One suspects that Aldous Huxley constructed his early novels with the aid of wheels bearing different neurotic types. He simply spun the circles until he found an amusing and explosive combination of house guests.) Mention also should be made of the book called *Plotto,* privately published in Battle Creek, Mich., 1928, by William Wallace Cook, a prolific writer of potboilers. Although *Plotto* did not use spinning wheels, it was essentially Lullian in its technique of combining plot elements, and apparently there were many writers willing to pay the seventy-five dollar price originally asked by the author.

In current philosophy one occasionally comes upon notions for which a Lullian device might be appropriate. For instance, Charles Morris tells us that a given sign (e.g., a word) can be analyzed in terms of three kinds of meaning: syntactic, semantic, and pragmatic. Each meaning in turn has a syntactic, semantic, and pragmatic meaning, and this threefold analysis can be carried on indefinitely. To dramatize this dialectical process one might use a series of rotating circles, each bearing the words "syntactic," "semantic," and "pragmatic," with the letter S in the center of the inner wheel to signify the sign being analyzed.

In science there also are rare occasions when a Lullian technique might prove useful. The tree diagram is certainly a convenient way to picture evolution. The periodic table can be considered a kind of Lullian chart that exhausts all permissible combinations of certain primitive principles and by means of which chemists have been able to predict the properties of elements before they were discovered. Lull's crude anticipation was a circle bearing the four traditional elements and rotated within a ring similarly labeled.

There may even be times when an inventor or researcher might find movable circles an aid. Experimental situations often call for a testing of all possible combinations of a limited number of substances or techniques. What is invention, after all, except the knack of finding new and useful combinations of old principles? When Thomas Edison systematically tested almost every available substance as a filament for his light bulb, he was following a process that Lull would probably have considered an extension of his method. One American scientist, an acoustical engineer and semiprofessional magician, Dariel Fitzkee, actually published in 1944 a book called *The Trick Brain* in which he explains a technique for combining ideas in Lullian fashion for the purpose of inventing new magic tricks.

If the reader will take the trouble to construct some Lullian circles related to a subject matter of special interest to himself, and play with them for a while, he will find it an effective way of getting close to Lull's mind. There is an undeniable fascination in twisting the wheels and letting the mind dwell on the strange combinations that turn up. Something of the mood of medieval Lullism begins to pervade the room and one comprehends for the first time why the Lullian cult persisted for so many centuries.

For persist it did.[10] Fifty years after Lull's death it was strong enough to provoke a vigorous campaign against Lullism, led by Dominican inquisitors. They succeeded in having Lull condemned as a heretic by a papal bull, though later church officials decided that the bull had been a forgery. Lullist schools, supported chiefly by Franciscans, flourished throughout the late Middle Ages and Renaissance, mostly in Spain but also in other parts of Europe. We have already cited Bruno's intense interest in the Art. The great ex-Dominican considered Lull's method divinely inspired though badly applied. For example, he thought Lull mad to suppose that such truths of faith as the incarnation and trinity could be established by necessary reasons. Bruno's first and last published works, as well as many in between, were devoted to correcting and improving the method, notably *The Compendious Building and Completion of the Lullian Art.*

In 1923 the British Museum acquired a portable sundial and compass made in Rome in 1593 in the form of a book (Figure 10).

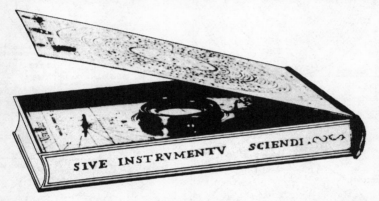

Figure 10. Sixteenth-century portable sundial engraved with Lullian figures. (From *Archaeologia*, Oxford, 1925.)

On the front and back of the two gilt copper "covers" are engraved the Lullian circles shown in Figures 11 to 14. For an explanation of these circles the reader is referred to O. M. Dalton's article, "A Portable Dial in the Form of a Book, with Figures Derived from Ramon Lul," *Archaeologia*, Vol. 74, second series, Oxford, 1925, pp. 89–102.

The seven smaller diagrams in Figure 12 are all from Lull's writings [11] and perhaps worth a few comments. The square in the upper left corner is designed to show how the mind can conceive of geometrical truths not apparent to the senses. A diagonal divides the square into two large triangles, one of which is subdivided to make the smaller triangles *B* and *C*. Each triangle contains three angles; so that our senses immediately perceive nine angles in all. However, we can easily imagine the large triangle to be subdi-

1. Upper cover, outer side

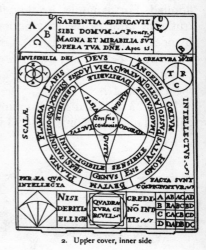

2. Upper cover, inner side

3. Lower cover, outer side

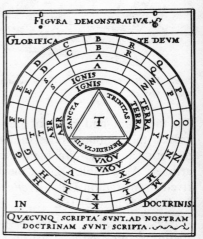

4. Lower cover, inner side

Figures 11 to 14, left to right, top to bottom. Circles used by Renaissance Lullists. (From *Archaeologia*, Oxford, 1925.)

vided also, making four small triangles or twelve angles in all. The three additional angles exist "potentially" in triangle A. We do not see them with our eyes, but we can see them with our imagination. In this way our intellect, aided by imagination, arrives at new geometrical truths.

The top right square is designed to prove that there is only one universe rather than a plurality of worlds. The two circles represent two universes. We see at once that certain parts of A and B are nearer to each other than other parts of A and B. But, Lull argues, "far" and "near" are meaningless concepts if nothing whatever exists in the space between A and B. We are forced to conclude that two universes are impossible.

I think what Lull means here, put in modern terms, is that we cannot conceive of two universes without supposing some sort of space-time relation between them, but once we relate them, we bring them into a common manifold; so we can no longer regard them as separate universes. Lull qualifies this by saying that his argument applies only to actual physical existence, not to higher realms of being which God could create at will, since His power is infinite.

The four intersecting circles are interesting because they anticipate in a vague way the use of circles to represent classes in the diagrammatic methods of Euler and Venn (to be discussed in the next chapter). The four letters which label the circles stand for *Esse* (being), *Unum* (the one), *Verum* (the true), and *Bonum* (the good). *Unum, verum,* and *bonum* are the traditional three "transcendentales" of scholastic philosophy. The overlapping of the circles indicates that the four qualities are inseparable. Nothing can exist without possessing unity, truth, and goodness.

The circle divided into three sectors represents the created universe, but I am not sure of the meaning of the letters which apparently signify the parts. The lower left square illustrates a practical problem in navigation. It involves a ship sailing east, but forced to travel in a strong north wind. The lower right square is clearly a Lullian table displaying the twelve permutations of *ABCD* taken two letters at a time.

The remaining diagram, at the middle of the bottom, is a primitive method of squaring the circle and one fairly common in medieval pseudo-mathematical works. We first inscribe a square and circumscribe a square; then we draw a third square midway between the other two. This third square, Lull mistakenly asserts, has a perimeter equal to the circumference of the circle as well as an area equal to the circle's area. Lull's discussion of this figure (in his *Ars magna et ultima*) reveals how far behind he was of the geometry of his time.[12] His method does not provide even a close approximation of the perimeter or area of the desired square.[13]

Books on the Lullian art proliferated throughout the seventeenth century, many of them carrying inserted sheets of circles to be cut out, or actual rotating circles with centers attached permanently to the page. Wildly exaggerated claims were made for the method. The German Jesuit Athanasius Kircher (1601–1680), scientist, mathematician, cryptographer, and student of Egyptian hieroglyphics, was also a confirmed Lullist. He published in Amsterdam in 1669 a huge tome of nearly 500 pages titled *Ars magna sciendi sive combinatoria*. It abounds with Lullian figures and circles bearing ingenious pictographic symbols of his own devising.[14]

The eighteenth century witnessed renewed opposition to Lull's teachings in Majorca and the publication of many Spanish books and pamphlets either attacking or defending him. Benito Feyjóo, in the second volume of his *Cartas eruditas y curiosas* ("Letters erudite and curious"), ridiculed Lull's art so effectively that he provoked a two-volume reply in 1749–1750 by the Cistercian monk Antonio Raymundo Pasqual, a professor of philosophy at the Lullian University of Majorca. This was followed in 1778 by Pasqual's *Vinciciae Lullianae,* an important early biography and defense of Lull. The nineteenth and twentieth centuries saw a gradual decline of interest in the Art and a corresponding increase of attention toward Lull as a poet and mystic. A periodical devoted to Lullian studies, the *Revista luliana,* flourished from 1901 to 1905. Today there are many enthusiastic admirers of Lull in Majorca and other parts of Spain, though the practice of his Art has all but completely vanished.[15]

The Church has approved Lull's beatification, but there seems little likelihood he will ever be canonized. There are three principal reasons. His books contain much that may be considered heretical. His martyrdom seems to have been provoked by such rash behavior that it takes on the coloration of a suicide. And finally, his insistence on the divine origin of his Art and his constant emphasis on its indispensability as a tool for the conversion of infidels lends a touch of madness, certainly of the fantastic, to Lull's personality. Lull himself was fully aware that his life was a fantastic one. He even wrote a book called *The Dispute of a Cleric and Ramon the Fantastic* in which he and a priest each try to prove that the other has had the most preposterous life. At other times he speaks of himself as "Ramon the Fool." He was indeed a Spanish *joglar* of the faith, a troubadour who sang his passionate love songs to his Beloved and twirled his colored circles as a juggler twirls his colored plates, more to the amusement or annoyance of his countrymen than to their edification. No one need regret that the controversy over his Great Art has at last been laid to rest and that the world is free to admire Lull as the first great writer in the Catalan tongue, and a religious eccentric unique in medieval Spanish history.

References

1. In later years Leibnitz was often critical of Lull, but he always regarded as sound the basic project sketched in his *Dissertio de arte combinatoria.* In a letter written in 1714 he makes the following comments:

    "When I was young, I found pleasure in the Lullian art, yet I thought also that I found some defects in it, and I said something about these in a little schoolboyish essay called *On the Art of Combinations,* published in 1666, and later reprinted without my permission. But I do not readily disdain anything—except the arts of divination, which are nothing but pure cheating—and I have found something valuable, too, in the art of Lully and in the *Digestum sapientiae* of the Capuchin, Father Ives, which pleased me greatly because he found a way to apply Lully's generalities to useful particular problems. But it seems to me that Descartes had a profundity of an entirely different level." (*Gottfried Wilhelm von Leibniz: Philosophical Papers and Letters,* edited and translated by Leroy E. Loemker, University of Chicago Press, 1956, Vol. 2, p. 1067.)

2. In sketching Lull's life I have relied almost entirely on E. Allison Peers's magnificent biography, *Ramon Lull,* London, 1929, the only adequate study of Lull in English. An earlier and briefer biography, *Raymond Lull, the Illuminated Doctor,* was published in London, 1904, by W. T. A. Barber, who also contributed an informative article on Lull to the *Encyclopedia of Religion and Ethics.* Other English references worth noting are: Otto Zöckler's article in the *Religious Encyclopedia;* William Turner's article in the *Catholic Encyclopedia;* George Sarton, *Introduction to the History of Science,* 1931, Vol. II, pp. 900 ff.; and Lynn Thorndike, *A History of Magic and Experimental Science,* 1923, Vol. II, pp. 862 ff.

    A voluminous bibliography of Lull's works, with short summaries of each, may be found in the *Histoire littéraire de la France,* Paris, 1885, Vol. XXIX, pp. 1–386, an indispensable reference for students of Lull. There also is an excellent article on Lull by P. Ephrem Langpré in Vol. IX of the *Dictionnaire de théologie Catholique,* Paris, 1927. It is interesting to note that a 420-page novel based on the life of Lull, *Le Docteur illumine,* by Lucien Graux, appeared in Paris in 1927.

The most accessible Spanish references are the articles on Lull in the *Enciclopedia universal ilustrada,* Barcelona, 1923, and Vol. 1 of *Historia de la filosofía española,* by Tomás Carreras y Artau, Madrid, 1939.

3. Quoted by Peers, *op. cit.,* p. 64.
4. An English translation by Peers was published in 1926.
5. Separately issued in English translation by Peers in 1923.
6. Lull's death is the basis of a short story by Aldous Huxley, "The Death of Lully," in his book *Limbo,* 1921.
7. The only satisfactory description in English of Lull's method is in Vol. 1 of Johann Erdmann's *History of Philosophy,* English translation, London, 1910. There are no English editions of any of Lull's books dealing with his Art. Peers's biography may be consulted for a list of Latin and Spanish editions of Lull's writings.
8. See *La logique de Leibniz,* by Louis Couturat, Paris, 1901, chap. IV, and *Leibniz,* by Ruth Lydia Shaw, London, 1954, chap. VIII.
9. Chapter 7 of my *Mathematics, Magic, and Mystery,* 1956, contains a reproduction and analysis of Loyd's "Get off the earth" puzzle and several related paradoxes.
10. *Historia del Lulisme,* by Joan Avinyó, a history of Lullism to the eighteenth century, was published in Barcelona in 1925. My quick survey of Lullism draws largely on Peers's account.
11. With the exception of the table of permutations, all these diagrams are reproduced and discussed in Zetzner's one-volume Latin edition of several of Lull's works, first printed in Strasbourg, 1598.
12. Bryson of Heraclea, a pupil of Socrates, had recognized that, if you keep increasing the number of sides of the inscribed and circumscribed polygons, you get increasingly closer approximations of the circle. It was through applying this method of limits that Archimedes was able to conclude that pi was somewhere between 3.141 and 3.142.

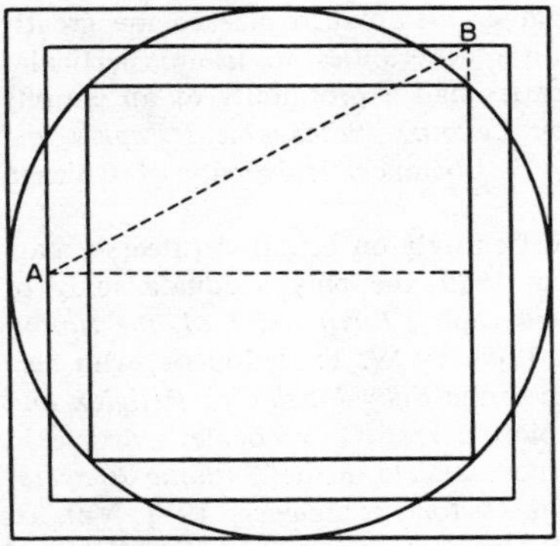

Figure 15.

13. It has been called to my attention that, if a diagonal line *AB* is drawn on Lull's figure as shown in Figure 15, it gives an extremely good approximation to the side of a square with an area equal to the area of the circle.
14. Kircher's enormous books are fascinating mixtures of science and nonsense. He seems to have anticipated motion pictures by constructing a magic lantern that threw images on a screen in fairly rapid succession to illustrate such events as the ascension of Christ. He invented (as did Leibnitz) an early calculating machine. On the other hand, he devoted a 250-page treatise to details in the construction of Noah's Ark!

Kircher's work on the Lullian art appeared three years after Leibnitz's youthful treatise of similar title (see reference 1). Leibnitz later wrote that he had hoped to find important matters discussed in Kircher's book but was disappointed to discover that it "had merely revived the Lullian art or something similar to it, but that the author had not even dreamed of the true analysis of human thoughts." (Vol. 1, p. 352, of the edition of Leibnitz's papers and letters cited in reference 1.)

15. Not entirely vanished! In recent decades there has been a revival of the Lullian art as a technique for creative thinking. Fritz Zwicky, an American astrophysicist, calls it the "morphological method." The basic scheme is to draw a picture of a box made up of cubical cells. If each coordinate axis is labeled with basic concepts related to a particular problem, each cubical cell represents a unique triplet of combinations of concepts. By meditating on these combinations, the mind is forced along strange paths in a way that is said to stimulate creativity. See Zwicky's book *Discovery, Invention, Research: Through the Morphological Approach*, Macmillan, 1969.

A more whimsical Lullian device called the Think Tank was widely advertised in 1975. For forty-five dollars you obtained a rotating plastic sphere filled with 13,000 tiny plastic chips. On each chip a word is printed. Rotating the tank causes the chips to tumble about. When you stop turning it, you see a set of unrelated words through a circular window. The idea is to make mental associations between these randomly selected words and whatever problem is at hand. The seeming irrelevance of each word breaks you away from "vertical" thinking into "lateral" thinking, thereby zig-zagging your thoughts in creative directions.

The Think Tank was invented and manufactured by Savo Bojicic, a Yugoslavian who settled in Canada. With the tank came a ninety-page booklet of instructions by Edward de Bono, a British author of numerous books on creativity. See "Yes, You Too Can Think Your Way to Greater Riches, Happiness and Success," by Alan Edmonds, in the Canadian periodical *Quest*, November, 1975, pp. 9–16.

2: Logic Diagrams

A logic diagram is a two-dimensional geometric figure with spatial relations that are isomorphic with the structure of a logical statement. These spatial relations are usually of a topological character, which is not surprising in view of the fact that logic relations are the primitive relations underlying all deductive reasoning and topological properties are, in a sense, the most fundamental properties of spatial structures. Logic diagrams stand in the same relation to logical algebras as the graphs of curves stand in relation to their algebraic formulas; they are simply other ways of symbolizing the same basic structure.

There has always been, and continues to be, a curious tendency among certain logicians to peer down their noses at logic diagrams as though they were barbaric attempts to picture a structure more appropriately represented by words or notational symbols. One might as well look upon the graph of a parabola as somehow of a lower status than the algebraic equation that produces it. Clearly, the parabola and its formula are simply two different ways of asserting the same thing. The parabola is a spatial way of representing an equation; the equation is an algebraic expression of a parabola. It would be foolish to ask which of the two, considered in itself, is superior to the other. Each has its uses, and it is only in reference to human purposes that we can speak of their relative merits or defects.

In logic, a good diagram has several virtues. Many individuals think with far greater ease when they can visualize an argument pictorially, and a diagram often makes clear to them a matter which they might have difficulty grasping in verbal or algebraic form. For this reason, logic diagrams are extremely valuable pedagogic devices. Moreover, a good diagrammatic method is capable of solving certain logic problems in the same efficient way that a graph may be used for the solution of certain equations. True—algebraic methods of dealing with logic problems are usually faster and more reliable, but this is not always the case, and even when it is, the diagram affords a convenient technique for checking results obtained by other means. Finally, the study of logic diagrams is an intensely interesting and relatively unexplored field. It is closely allied with the rapidly growing subject of topology, and its kinship with the network theory underlying the construction of electronic calculators and other automata suggests that it may have contributions to make in the near future that will be much more than trivial or recreational.

Historically, the first logic diagrams probably expressed statements in what today is called the logic of relations. The tree figure, for example, was certainly known to Aristotle as a handy way of picturing successive subdivisions of matter and form, or genera and species. The so-called tree of Porphyry, so often found in medieval and Renaissance logics, is one example of this type of diagram. In the previous chapter we spoke of Lull's fondness for the tree device, and its useful application today in depicting such structures as the evolutionary history of plants and animals. The genealogical family tree (actually an interlocking of many separate tree figures) is another example. Drawing such a tree is often the quickest and easiest way to determine a relationship between two people, another way of saying that it is a useful tool for solving a certain type of logic problem.

Statements involving transitive asymmetric relations, such as "taller than," "heavier than," "to the left of," and so on, are so easily diagramed that the technique must have been a familiar one to the ancients, certainly so obvious as to be of little interest to us here. Likewise, we may pass quickly over such popular medieval devices as the various "squares of opposition" (for showing certain relations of immediate inference from one class proposition to another) as well as the "pons asinorum" of Petrus Tartaretus. The latter is a geometrical method of finding the middle terms of an argument. Jean Buridan, the fourteenth century French nominalist, was much concerned in his logical writings with finding middle terms, and his method became known as a "pons asinorum" ("bridge of asses") because it helped dull-witted students pass over from the major and minor terms to the middle ones. The phrase later became attached to the elaborate hexagonal figure that apparently first appeared in a fifteenth century work on logic by Petrus Tartaretus. (The interested reader will find the figure reproduced and explained in Karl Prantl's *Geschichte der Logik im Abendlande*, Leipzig, 1855–1870, Vol. 4, p. 206.) In later centuries, pons asinorum became a common phrase for Euclid's fifth proposition proving the base angles of an isosceles triangle to be equal, a bridge that only stupid students had difficulty in crossing.

On a slightly higher "iconic" level (Charles Peirce's term for the resemblance of a sign to the thing it signifies) are the three diagrams pictured in Figure 16. These are designed to exhibit the rela-

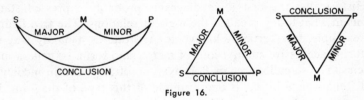

Figure 16.

tions between terms in the first three figures of a syllogism. William Hamilton, in *Discussions on Philosophy and Literature,* 1866, p. 666, traces their origin back to the fifth century of the Christian era. They are to be found in Lull's logical works and innumerable other medieval treatises. Giordano Bruno, in a commentary on Lull's system, superimposes the three figures and surrounds them

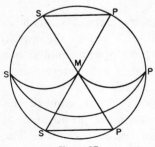

Figure 17.

with a circle to obtain the mysterious diagram shown in Figure 17. Beyond showing that the conclusion of a syllogism expresses a relation between two terms that is obtained by traversing another route that leads through a middle term, these figures have almost no iconic value and need not detain us further.

The first important step toward a diagrammatic method sufficiently iconic to be serviceable as a tool for solving problems of class logic was the use of a simple closed curve to represent a class. We have seen how Lull employed four intersecting circles to show that existence possesses the transcendental predicates of truth, goodness, and unity. The use of three intersecting circles to illustrate the unity of the three parts of the godhead was also a common medieval figure. It is difficult to say who was the first to use a circle for representing actual class propositions and syllogisms. Alonzo Church, in his contribution to the section on logic in the fourteenth edition of the Encyclopaedia Britannica, mentions the early use of circles for this purpose by Johann Christoph Sturm (in his *Universalia Euclidea,* 1661), Leibnitz, and Johann Christian Lange (in his *Nucleus logicae Weisianae,* 1712). There is no doubt, however, that it was Leonhard Euler, the brilliant Swiss mathematician, who was responsible for introducing them into the history of logical analysis. He first described them in seven letters, the earliest written in 1761, and all printed in his *Lettres à une princesse d'Allemagne,* Vol. 2, 1772, letters 102 to 108. Here for the first time we meet with a geometrical system that will not only represent class statements and syllogisms in a highly isomorphic manner, but also can be manipulated for the actual solution of problems in class logic.

Euler's method will not be explained here because it has been supplanted by the much more efficient method developed by the English logician John Venn (1834–1923), lecturer in the moral sciences, Cambridge University. Venn's *Symbolic Logic,* revised second edition, 1894, may be consulted for a clear exposition of Euler's system as well as an analysis of its defects. In the last chapter of Venn's book one will also find a compact survey of the history of class logic diagrams, a survey from which much of the foregoing data have been drawn. This chapter may also be consulted for interesting anticipations of Euler's system, as well as later variations that employ triangles, squares, and other parallelograms. Since class inclusion is not concerned with numerical quantity, any closed curve topologically equivalent to a circle can be used. Of special interest is a linear method of diagraming, closely allied to the Euler circles, that was developed by Euler's contemporary, the German mathematician Johann Heinrich Lambert, and explained in his *Neues Organon,* 1764.[1]

All these methods, including Euler's, had severe limitations. They were elegantly overcome by Venn's system of intersecting circles, which explains why they have dropped into such complete oblivion. Venn first published his method in an article, "On the Diagrammatic and Mechanical Representation of Propositions and Reasonings," *Philosophical Magazine,* July, 1880. The technique is discussed more fully in his book cited above.

There are several aspects of the "Venn circles" that will be of interest to consider in this chapter, but before doing so it will be expedient to digress for a moment and consider briefly the nature of the syllogism. This discussion will have an important bearing on much that follows, as well as make it easier to understand the syllogism-solving machines to be described in later chapters.

Although Aristotle defined the syllogism broadly as any formal argument in which the conclusion follows necessarily from the premises, his own analysis centers on a very specific type of argument. He had observed that statements often took a subject-predicate form with the subject preceded by such qualifying adjectives as "all," "some," "none." The four most common statements of this type, traditionally labeled *A, E, I,* and *O,* are:

> *A*—All *S* is *P* (universal affirmative)
> *E*—No *S* is *P* (universal negative)
> *I*—Some *S* is *P* (particular affirmative)
> *O*—Some *S* is not *P* (particular negative)

Aristotle further observed that a statement of this sort could be correctly inferred from two statements of similar form, one relating the subject (*S*) of the conclusion to a "middle term" (*M*), the other relating the middle term to the predicate (*P*) of the conclusion. For example:

> All *M* is *P*
> All *S* is *M*
> All *S* is *P*

It was this specific type of "mediate inference" by way of a middle term that Aristotle was the first to dissect and analyze, and to which the term "syllogism" soon became firmly attached. Aristotle's way of classifying syllogisms was to divide them into three "figures" depending on the "width" or "extension" of the middle term (i.e., whether it concerned all or part of its class) as compared with the width of the other terms. Later logicians, classifying syllogisms by the *position* of the middle term, added a fourth figure. Each figure in turn was divided into "moods," each mood being a different combination of the four basic statements. The syllogism cited above is in the mood *AAA* of the first figure. Medieval logicians gave a mnemonic name to each valid syllogism, the vowels of the name corresponding to the three assertions of the syllogism. In this case the mnemonic name is *Barbara*.

If we assume that every term in a syllogism stands for a class that actually has members (e.g., when a premise asserts that "All unicorns have only one horn," we must assume that there are such things as unicorns), then 24 of the 256 combinations are valid inferences. Only 15 are valid if we adopt the narrower view that a class qualified by "all" or "none" may be "empty"; that is, it may or may not have members.

It is true of course that Aristotle and his medieval followers greatly exaggerated the importance of the syllogism. In the light of modern symbolic logic we now see it as a restricted form of class-inclusion inference seldom encountered in everyday thought or speech. The following quotation from Bertrand Russell's *An Outline of Philosophy*, 1927, is a well-known expression of the disdain a modern logician feels for this ancient logical form:

This form of inference does actually occur, though very rarely. The only instance I have ever heard of was supplied by Dr. F. C. S. Schiller. He once produced a comic number of the philosophical periodical *Mind*, and sent copies to various philosophers, among others to a certain German, who was much puzzled by the advertisements. But at last he argued: "Everything in this book is a joke, therefore the advertisements are jokes." I have never come across any other case of new knowledge obtained by means of a syllogism. It must be admitted that, for a method which dominated logic for two thousand years, this contribution to the world's stock of information cannot be considered very weighty.

In the confused period that followed the Renaissance break with the logic of the schoolmen, and before Boole and others cleared the way for the development of symbolic logic, it was natural that logicians would make every conceivable attempt to reconstruct the syllogism or extend it to cover new forms of inference. Francis Bacon spoke of the syllogism as having "been beaten over and over by the subtlest labors of men's wits." Now it came in for another round of drubbing until it was almost pounded out of recognizable shape. What was needed, of course, was a broader point of view and an adequate system of symbolic notation. But until these needs were met, logicians expended an incredible amount of energy in verbal experimentation and argument. Perhaps these were necessary preliminaries to algebraic analysis, but looking back on them now they seem, especially the labors of the nineteenth century German metaphysicians, trivial and often hilarious.

Christoph von Sigwart, for instance, thought that syllogisms should be expressed in a hypothetical form: If anything is M it is P; if anything is S it is M; therefore if anything is S it is P. Franz Brentano's "existential syllogism" put all affirmative statements into a negative form: There is not a not-mortal human; there is not a not-human Socrates; therefore there is not a not-mortal Socrates. Wilhelm Schuppe decided that Aristotle was mistaken when he said that no conclusion could be derived from two negative premises. For can we not reason: No M is P; no S is M; therefore neither S nor M is P? And if that didn't prove the point, Schuppe had another example: No M is P; no S is M; therefore S *may* be P. Of course S may be P even without the premises, and in either case it may also not be P. Nevertheless we can say for certain that we cannot say for certain anything about the relation of S to P. Schuppe felt that this should be recognized as a kind of conclusion.

Schuppe also believed, contrary to traditional rules, that a conclusion could be obtained from two particular premises. Thus: Some M is P; some S is M; therefore some S may be P. Another Schuppe syllogism, much discussed by European logicians in his day, ran: All P is M; all S is M; therefore S is in some respect similar to P. What Schuppe meant was that S and P have in common the fact that both of them have certain attributes of M. If all dimes are round and all wheels are round, then wheels and dimes are similar in their roundness. One would have thought that only the German philosophers would be impressed by this discovery; nevertheless in England the great Bosanquet thought highly of it.

The most famous of these endless attempts to reshape or enlarge the Aristotelian syllogism was the "quantification of the predicate" by the Scottish philosopher Sir William Hamilton (1788–1856). Hamilton correctly perceived, as Leibnitz and many others had before him, that the predicate term in each of Aristotle's four basic assertions (A,E,I,O) is ambiguous in the sense that it does not tell us whether we are concerned with all or part of the predicate. Why not, Hamilton asked himself, increase the precision of these four statements by quantifying their predicates? In other words, for the ambiguous "All S is P" we substitute the two fully quantified assertions, "All S is *all P*" and "All S is *some P*." The old logic would treat "All men are mortal" and "All men are featherless bipeds" as identical in form; whereas in the new system we see at once that the first statement is an example of "All S is *some P* (all men are *some* mortals) and the second is an example of "All S is *all P*" (all men are *all* featherless bipeds). Since each of the four traditional statements can be replaced by two with quantified predicates, we have eight basic propositions out of which to construct syllogisms. They combine to form 512 possible moods of which 108 prove to be valid.

Let us say at once that there is no reason at all why the predicate should not be quantified. The trouble is that in doing so we are beginning to break so completely with the way in which common speech expresses class relations that, unless we develop a really complete and precise system of notation, we find ourselves forced to employ words in a clumsy and barbarous way. This was one of the criticisms of Hamilton's system voiced by his contemporary, the English mathematician Augustus De Morgan (1806–1871). De Morgan found among Hamilton's valid moods a syllogism with such cloudy phrasing that it seemed to assert that all men who were not lawyers were made of stone. De Morgan dubbed it the "Gorgon syllogism" and there was much heated British debate about it on the part of pro and anti Hamiltonians.

Hamilton attempted to remedy the obscurity of his phrasing by devising a curious system of notation that should be mentioned here because it has the superficial appearance of a diagram. Actually, there is no attempt to find a spatial analogue of classes. The system consists only of symbols with agreed-upon meanings, and rather cumbersome symbols at that in spite of Hamilton's own opinion that they were "easy, simple, compendious, all-sufficient, consistent, manifest, precise, and complete." The system employed the English C and the Greek capital gamma (each the third letter in its alphabet) for the two terms of the conclusion, and M for the middle term of the premises. The affirmative copula ("is" or "are") is a wedge-shaped line with its thick end toward the subject. It can be made negative by a vertical line crossing it at the center. A colon is used to signify a distributed (universal) term, a comma to signify an undistributed (particular) term. As an example, Figure 18 shows how Hamilton recorded the syllogism *Barbara*.

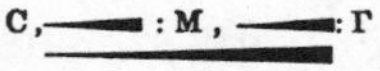

C,———:M,———:Γ

Figure 18.

Hamilton also used his wedge-shaped marks to form triangular designs representing the three Aristotelian figures, superimposing them to produce a pattern (Figure 19) even more mysterious than

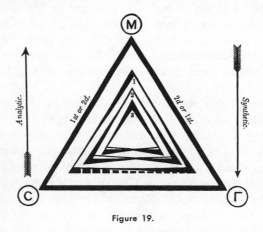

Figure 19.

Bruno's similar effort. The outside triangle, with boundary lines of even width, represents Hamilton's "unfigured syllogism." This was another of the Scottish philosopher's innovations. By transforming the phrasing of any valid syllogism with quantified predicates, he was able to express it in statements of equality. For example:

> All men and some mortals are equal.
> Socrates and some (in this case, one) men are equal.
> Socrates and some (one) mortals are equal.

Some logicians are of the opinion that this was Hamilton's only significant contribution to logic, because it suggested that logical statements might be reduced to something analogous to algebraic equations and so gave encouragement to those who were seeking a suitable algebraic notation. Unfortunately, Hamilton failed to comprehend even the most elementary mathematical concepts, and although his logical system has a neat verbal symmetry, it proved to be virtually useless in practice. In common speech, for instance, if one says "Some of Picasso's paintings are mediocre," one does not *want* to quantify the predicate, it being obvious that there are other mediocre things that are not paintings by Picasso. It is one of the peculiar virtues of the traditional system that it is constructed from intentionally ambiguous statements such as occur in common discourse, whereas in Hamilton's system, to make a statement with an ambiguous predicate becomes an exceedingly complicated matter.

De Morgan also quantified the predicate in a system even more elaborate than Hamilton's. By allowing subject and predicate terms to have both positive and negative forms, he arrived at thirty-two basic statements, though many of them are merely different ways of saying the same thing. Hamilton accused De Morgan of plagiarism, and for many years the two men argued with each other in books and magazine articles—perhaps the bitterest and funniest debate about formal logic since the time of the schoolmen, though most of the humor as well as insight was on the side of De Morgan. They fought, De Morgan once recalled, like a cat and dog, "one dogmatical, the other categorical." De Morgan always maintained that he deliberately softened his verbal fire because of Hamilton's ill health, though at times he suspected that replying to Hamilton in the same abusive tone Hamilton employed might have given the ailing metaphysician a beneficial shot in the arm.

De Morgan's many contributions to logic, owing to his mathematical skill, proved more fruitful than Hamilton's, though not so fruitful as the work of Boole. In his *Budget of Paradoxes,* Book I, pp. 333 ff., De Morgan summarized his work under six heads, each propounding a new type of syllogism—relative, undecided, exemplar, numerical, onzymatic, and transposed. His example of a relative syllogism is: X is the brother of Y; X is not the uncle of Z; therefore Z is not the child of Y. An undecided syllogism: some men are not capable of tracing consequences; we cannot be sure that there are beings responsible for consequences who are incapable of tracing consequences; therefore we cannot be sure that all men are responsible for the consequences of their actions. The term "exemplar" refers, De Morgan writes, to a system he worked

38

out for the purpose of correcting defects in Hamilton's logic, but which turned out to be the same as Aristotle's.

De Morgan's numerical syllogism is of special interest because it shows how easily traditional class logic slides over into arithmetic. He gives two examples, the first of which is: most Y's are X's; most Y's are Z's; therefore some X's are Z's. The second example presupposes that 100 Y's exist. We can now reason: 70 X's are Y's; 40 Z's are Y's; therefore at least 10 X's are Z's. Boole, Jevons, and many other pioneers of modern logic discussed syllogisms of this type at considerable length. "Onzymatic" refers to De Morgan's expansion of the Aristotelian system by the use of negative terms and quantified predicates (see his *Syllabus of a Proposed System of Logic,* 1860). As an example of a transposed syllogism he cites: some X's are not Y's; for every X there is a Y which is Z; therefore some Z's are not X's.

The initial letters of the names of these six new varieties of syllogism, De Morgan points out, can be arranged to spell "Rue not!" indicating his unrepentance for having invented them. He adds, however, that followers of the old logic can take comfort from the fact that the same letters can be transposed to spell "True? No!"

All these strange forms and extensions of the syllogism so far mentioned (and they are but a fraction of the pseudo-syllogisms proposed by various logicians of the last century) are of little interest to a modern logician. They were courageous verbal attempts to extend the domain of formal logic beyond its traditional boundaries, but from the standpoint of modern symbolic logic they appear obvious and uninteresting. Some are merely new verbal ways of making an old assertion, like saying that 8 minus 3 equals 5 instead of saying 5 plus 3 equals 8. Others put into a syllogistic form a type of inference quite different from that involved in an Aristotelian syllogism. Such forms may be perfectly valid but they no more constitute a criticism or reform of the traditional syllogism than the theorems of non-Euclidean geometry can be said to criticize or reform the Pythagorean theorem. We now know that Aristotle's syllogism is only one of an infinite variety of forms of inference, but within its own domain it does exactly what it is supposed to do. Leibnitz thought it was "one of the most beautiful inventions of the human spirit," and there is no reason why a logician today need disagree, even though he finds the syllogism's structure no longer a field for further exploration.

It was of course the development of an adequate symbolic notation that reduced the syllogism to triviality and rendered obsolete all the quasi-syllogisms that had been so painfully and exhaustively analyzed by the nineteenth century logicians. At the same time, many a controversy that once seemed important no longer seemed so. Few logicians care today whether a syllogism is or is not reduced to the first figure, or whether we should recognize three figures or four. Perhaps one reason why these old issues faded so quickly was that, shortly after Boole laid the foundations for an algebraic notation, John Venn came forth with an ingenious improvement on Euler's circles. The result was a diagrammatic method so perfectly isomorphic with the Boolean class algebra, and picturing the structure of class logic with such visual clarity, that even a nonmathematically minded philosopher could "see" what the new logic was all about.

To understand exactly how Venn's method works, let us apply it first to a syllogism. We begin by drawing three circles that intersect like the trade-mark of Ballantine's ale (Figure 20). The circles are labeled S (subject), M (middle term), and P (predicate). All the points inside circle S are regarded as members of class S. All points outside the same circle are regarded as not-S. (In this book we shall adopt the convention of symbolizing a negation by placing a $\sim$ before the term: $\sim S$.) The same applies to the other circles. As we see by inspection, the circles overlap in such a way that, if we label each compartment with appropriate letters to indicate its members, we shall have a compartment for every possible three-term combination of the three letters and their negations (Figure 21). The region outside all three circles will represent the region of $\sim S \sim M \sim P$, or all those things that are not members of any of the three classes singled out for consideration.

The following conventions must be adopted. If we wish to show that a compartment is empty (has no members) we shade it. If we wish to show that it has members, we place a small X inside it. If we do not know whether an X belongs in one compartment or an adjacent one, we put it on the border between the two areas.

Let us now diagram the premise "All S is M." We interpret this to mean that the class of things which are S and $\sim M$ is empty;

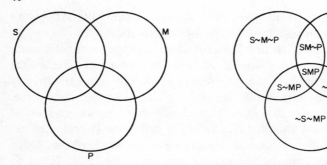

Figure 20.   Figure 21.

therefore we shade all compartments in which we find these two terms (Figure 22).

Our second premise, let us say, is "No *M* is *P*." This clearly asserts that all compartments containing the combination *MP* are empty. So we shade the diagram further, as shown in Figure 23.

At this point we must inspect the circles to see if we can draw a valid conclusion concerning the relation of *S* to *P*. We can. All areas containing both *S* and *P* are empty; hence we conclude "No *S* is *P*." If we assume that *S* is not an empty class, we may also conclude (since only one compartment in *S* is not shaded) that "Some *S* is not *P*." (This is called a "weak" conclusion because it may be derived by immediate inference from a universal or "stronger" conclusion, "No *S* is *P*.")

One more illustration is needed to make clear how particular premises are handled. "Some *S* is *M*" requires an *X* on the border of the *P* circle as shown in Figure 24, because we do not know which of the two compartments (or perhaps both) may have members. If our next premise is "All *M* is *P*" it will eliminate one of these compartments, allowing us to shift the *X* to the non-empty area as shown in Figure 25. Inspection now reveals that from the two premises we may validly conclude that "Some *S* is *P*."

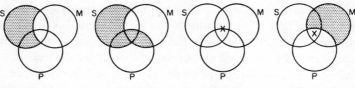

Figure 22.   Figure 23.   Figure 24.   Figure 25.

What we have been doing, in a sense, is to translate the verbal symbols of a syllogism into a problem of topology. Each circle is a closed curve, and according to the "Jordan theorem" of topology a closed curve must divide all points on the plane into those which are inside and those which are outside the curve. The points inside each circle constitute a distinct "set" or "class" of points. We thus have a simple geometrical model by means of which we can show exactly which points lie within or without a given set. The question now arises, do the topological laws involved here underlie the logic of class inclusion, or do the laws of class inclusion underlie the topological laws? It is clearly a verbal question. Neither underlies the other. We have in the Venn circles and in the syntax of a syllogism two different ways of symbolizing the same structure— one grammatical, the other geometrical. Neither, as Peirce expresses it, is "the cause or principle of the other."

A word or two now about how the circles may be used for showing class propositions linked by a disjunctive ("or") relation. Suppose we wish to say that all X is either Y or Z, taking "or" in

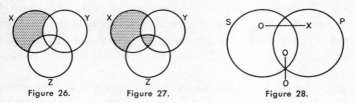

Figure 26.   Figure 27.   Figure 28.

the inclusive sense of "either or both." Figure 26 shows how simply this is done. To change this to an "exclusive" disjunction ("either but not both") we have only to shade the central area as shown in Figure 27. More complex disjunctive statements, jointly asserted, require other stratagems. Peirce suggested (*Collected Papers,* Vol. 4, pp. 307ff.) a simple way that this could be done. It involves the use of X's and O's to stand for presence or absence of members, then connecting them by a line to indicate disjunction. For example, Figure 28 shows how Peirce diagramed the statement "Either all S is P or some P is not-S, and either no S is P or no not-S is not-P."

Hypothetical class statements such as "If all A is B then all B is C," and other types of compound statements, do not readily admit of diagraming. The best procedure seems to be, following another suggestion of Peirce's (*op. cit.,* p. 315), to draw Venn diagrams of Venn diagrams. We shall see how this is done when we consider, later in the chapter, the use of the Venn circles for depicting truth-value statements in the propositional calculus.

It is interesting to note that, by changing at least one of the circles to a rectangle, the Venn diagram easily takes care of numerical syllogisms in which terms are quantified by "most" or by numbers. Figure 29 shows how one can diagram the syllogism: there are ten

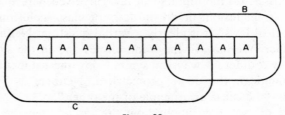

Figure 29.

A's of which four are *B*'s; eight *A*'s are *C*'s; therefore at least two *B*'s are *C*'s. Some elementary problems of probability also lend themselves to this type of diagram. Peirce suggested a different method of using circles for problems involving numerically quantified classes (*op. cit.,* p. 315), but his proposal is more notational than diagrammatic.

One of the merits of the Venn system is that it can be extended in principle to take care of any number of terms. The simplest way to provide for four terms is to use ellipses as shown in Figure 30 (it being impossible to make four circles intersect on a plane in the desired manner). The following problem, taken from Venn's *Symbolic Logic,* will suffice to indicate the scope and power of the method.

> Every *Y* is either *X* and not *Z,* or *Z* and not *X.*
> Every *WY* is either both *X* and *Z* or neither of the two.
> All *XY* is either *W* or *Z,* and all *YZ* is either *X* or *W.*

If we diagram these statements properly, as shown in Figure 31, we see at once the surprising conclusion. The premises make it impossible for any *Y* to exist.

As the number of terms increases, the diagram of course becomes more involved. It is possible to draw any number of closed curves that intersect in the necessary manner, but beyond four it is difficult to devise diagrams that permit the eye to grasp quickly the spots that are inside or outside a given curve. The more terms involved, the more peculiar become the shapes of the curves.[2] For five terms, Venn proposed the diagram shown in Figure 32. This has, however, the defect of giving class Z the shape of a doughnut, the small ellipse in the center being *outside* Z but inside W and Y. Beyond five terms, Venn thought it best to abandon hope of keep-

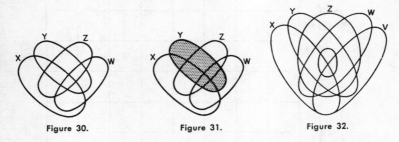

Figure 30.   Figure 31.   Figure 32.

ing all parts of one class within a closed curve, and simply to divide a rectangle into the desired number of subcompartments, labeling each with a different combination of the terms.

The first published suggestion for a rectangular graph of this sort was an article titled "A Logical Diagram for *n* Terms," by Allan Marquand, then a fellow at Johns Hopkins University. It appeared in the *Philosophical Magazine,* Vol. 12, October, 1881, p. 266. As we shall see in Chapter 6, Marquand also made use of this graph in the construction of his logic machine. Figure 33 pictures a Marquand graph for six terms. The square marked X indicates the class $\sim AB \sim C \sim DEF$. By shading areas asserted empty, and marking with an X the areas known to have members, problems involving six terms can be solved in the same manner as with Venn circles. This type of graph, like Lambert's system of linear diagraming, lies on the border line between a highly iconic system such as Venn's, and a noniconic system of notation. It reminds us that there is no sharp line separating symbolic notation from a diagram. Even algebraic notation is in some degree iconic, if only in the fact that single symbols stand for single terms, and even the most iconic diagram must make use of some conventions of a noniconic nature.

44

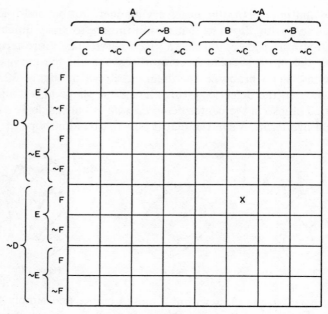

Figure 33.

Other types of graphs capable of extension to *n* terms have been proposed. Alexander Macfarlane, a professor of physics at the University of Texas, abandoned the square graph for a long narrow strip subdivided as shown in Figure 34. Macfarlane called this a "logical spectrum." Null classes are indicated by gray shading. Compartments excluded by the premises are shaded black.

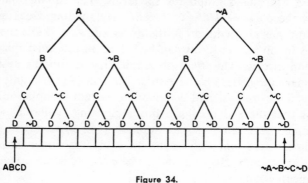

Figure 34.

Indeterminate classes are indicated by shading half the compartment black. The system was first explained in an article titled "The Logical Spectrum," *Philosophical Magazine*, Vol. 19, 1885, p. 286. In the *Proceedings of the American Association for the Advancement of Science,* Vol. 39, 1890, p. 57, in a paper titled "Adaptation of the Method of the Logical Spectrum to Boole's Problem," Macfarlane showed how easily his diagram solved an involved problem posed by Boole on p. 146 of his *Laws of Thought.*[3]

A method of dividing a square, somewhat different from Marquand's, was proposed by William J. Newlin, of Amherst College, in an article titled "A New Logical Diagram," *Journal of Philosophy, Psychology, and Scientific Methods,* Vol. 3, Sept. 13, 1906, p. 539. Still another rectangular method was suggested by the distinguished Harvard philosopher William E. Hocking in one of his rare moments of concern with formal logic. Hocking's paper, "Two Extensions of the Use of Graphs in Elementary Logic," appeared in the *University of California Publications in Philosophy,* Vol. 2, No. 2, 1909, p. 31.

Another interesting Marquand-type graph, using colored counters to indicate presence or absence of class members, was invented by Lewis Carroll and first explained in his delightfully written little book, *The Game of Logic,* 1886. The game, Carroll tells us in his preface, requires one player *at least.* Purchasers of the book also received an envelope containing a card with Carroll's diagram, to be used as a board for the game, and nine cardboard counters (four red and five gray). This card is reproduced in Figure 35.

The large square on the card is so divided that its areas represent all three-term combinations of X, Y, M and their negations (Carroll adopts the convention of using an apostrophe to indicate negation). The upper half of this square is $X;$ the lower half is X' (not-X). The left side of the square is Y, the right side Y'. M (the middle term, for Carroll is here concerned only with the syllogism) is indicated by the space inside the interior square. M' is the area between this inner square and the outer border of the diagram.

To diagram the premises of a syllogism we simply mark the appropriate compartments with counters—a red counter for spaces known to contain members, a gray counter for spaces known to be empty. If we know that at least one of two adjacent compartments has members, but are not sure which one, the red counter is placed on the border between the two areas. After we have suitably marked the graph in accord with our premises, inspection of the diagram will give us the conclusion, if any, that we may reach

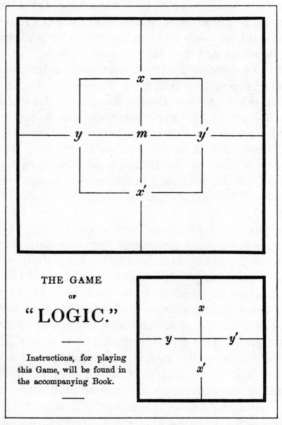

Figure 35. Reproduction of the board used in playing Lewis Carroll's logic game.

concerning the relation of X to Y. The smaller square in the lower right corner of the card is used merely for recording the conclusion.

Carroll's diagram, like that of Venn and the various extensions of Venn's method, easily takes care of syllogisms with mixtures of positive and negative forms of the same term. In traditional logic such statements would have to be rephrased to arrive at a valid syllogistic form. For example, consider the following typically Carrollian problem:

> All teetotalers like sugar.
> No nightingale drinks wine.

If we substitute letters for the terms we have:

> All *M* are *X*
> No *Y* is not-*M*

By placing the counters according to Carroll's conventions, we quickly discover that we may draw the valid conclusion "No *Y* is not-*X*" or "No nightingale dislikes sugar." Carroll himself points out that traditional logicians would not admit this to be a valid syllogism (although as we have seen, De Morgan and others included such forms in their expansions of the traditional logic). "They have a sort of nervous dread," Carroll writes, "of Attributes beginning with a negative particle. . . . And thus, having (from sheer nervousness) excluded a quantity of very useful forms, they have made rules which, though quite applicable to the few forms which they allow of, are of no use at all when you consider all possible forms."

"Let us not quarrel with them, dear Reader!" Carroll continues. "There is room enough in the world for both of us. Let us quietly take our broader system: and, if they choose to shut their eyes to all these useful forms, and to say 'They are not Syllogisms at all!' we can but stand aside, and let them Rush upon their Fate!"

In a later book, *Symbolic Logic,* 1896 (reissued in 1955 by Dover Publications and Berkeley Enterprises), Carroll explained his diagrammatic method in greater detail, distinguishing it from the systems of Euler and Venn in the following characteristic manner:

My Method of Diagrams *resembles* Mr. Venn's, in having separate Compartments assigned to the various Classes, and in marking these Compartments as *occupied* or as *empty;* but it *differs* from his Method, in assigning a *closed* area to the *Universe of Discourse,* so that the Class which, under Mr. Venn's liberal sway, has been ranging at will through Infinite Space, is suddenly dismayed to find itself "cabin'd, cribb'd, confined," in a limited Cell like any other Class!

Apparently Carroll was not familiar with Marquand's earlier proposed diagram, because it likewise assigns a closed area to the

48

region outside of the classes under consideration. Carroll's graph, also like Marquand's, can be extended to *n* terms. *Symbolic Logic* pictures a number of these extensions, including a 256-cell graph for eight terms. The frontispiece of this book, reproduced in Figure

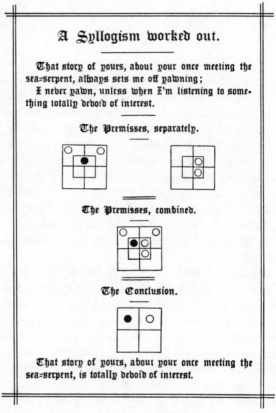

Figure 36. Frontispiece of Lewis Carroll's *Symbolic Logic*, 1886.

36, shows how the counters are placed to solve a syllogism about a sea-serpent story that induces yawning.

All the foregoing methods of diagraming class-inclusion logic were developed before the modern truth-value propositional calculus assumed its present form and importance. As we have seen, the terms of class logic stand for classes. In the propositional calculus, terms stand for statements (such as "It is raining") which may be regarded as true or false, and which are logically related by such "connectives" as "and," "or," "not," "both," "if . . . then." The question naturally arises, can these diagrams be used for solving problems in the propositional calculus? The answer is yes, as Venn himself recognized though he did not elaborate the technique. In fact, if the premises are not complicated by compound (parenthetical) assertions, the Venn diagrams can be used with surprising efficiency.

The propositional calculus first arose, it is worth recalling, as an interpretation of the class calculus. The correspondence between the two calculi is so close that every class statement has a corresponding propositional form. For example, "All A is B" can be interpreted to mean, "If X is a member of class A, then X is a member of class B." Similarly, "If A is true then B is true" may be interpreted to mean, "The class of all occasions on which A is true is included in the class of occasions on which B is true." "If it rains, I stay indoors," is a truth-value assertion. But if I say the same thing differently, "All rainy days are days when I stay indoors," it becomes a class statement. Every statement in truth-function logic has a similar class analogue. As the diagraming of these statements will make clear, they are simply different verbal ways of stating the same underlying logical structure.

To use the Venn circles for propositional logic we must first interpret them in a different way. Each circle now stands for a proposition which may be either true or false, rather than a class which may or may not have members. The labels on the various compartments (Figure 37) indicate possible or impossible combinations of true and false values of the respective terms. Just as we formerly shaded a compartment to show that it had no members, we now shade it to indicate that it is an impossible combination of truth values. Conversely, an unshaded compartment indicates a permissible combination. (Note in Figure 37 that the combination $\sim A \sim B \sim C$ is shown as a small circle outside the other three. This is done to simplify the shading, when necessary, of this area.)

If we wish to show that A is true, we shade all compartments containing $\sim A$ (Figure 38). To show that A is false, we shade all areas containing A (Figure 39).

A and $\sim A$ are of course negations of each other. Their dia-

50

grams are like positive and negative prints; to change from one to
the other we have only to exchange black and white areas. This
is one of the delightful features of the method. The diagram of
any truth-value assertion can be converted to its negation by following this simple procedure.

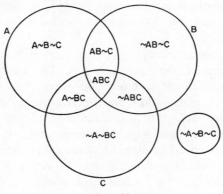

Figure 37.

Let us see how we go about depicting a statement of implica-
tion, "If A is true, then B is true" (symbolized as $A \supset B$). A truth
table for this relation tells us there are four possible true and false
combinations ($TT, TF, FT,$ and FF) of which only the combination TF is invalid. Hence we eliminate all compartments containing
$A \sim B$. The result (shown in Figure 40) is, as we would expect, a
diagram identical with the diagram for the class statement, "All A
is B."

The nature of "material implication" is easily explained by this
figure. If we add to it the statement that A is false (by shading all
unshaded areas containing A) it will appear as in Figure 39.
The white areas in this diagram tell us that B may be either true
or false. In other words, a false proposition "implies" any proposition, true or false. On the other hand, if we make A true (Figure

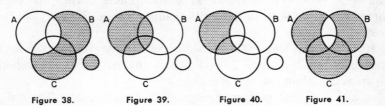

Figure 38.　　　Figure 39.　　　Figure 40.　　　Figure 41.

41), we see immediately that B must be true. Any true proposition, therefore, implies any other true one.

Figure 42 introduces the notational symbols that will be used throughout this book for all binary (two-term) truth-value relations for which there are commonly used symbols. The diagram for each relation is shown on the left. On the right is the "negative" diagram for the negation of each relation.

To apply these diagrams to relations between B and C, we have only to rotate the page until the A and B circles correspond to the positions of the B and C circles. In the same way we can turn the page to bring the A and B circles to the positions of C and A. After we work with the diagrams for a while, the patterns are soon memorized and problems involving no more than three terms can be solved with great speed. After a time, elementary problems of this sort can even be solved in the head. One has only to form a mental picture of the circles, then perform on them the necessary shadings. Both Venn and Carroll, incidentally, wrote of the ease with which they learned to solve logic problems mentally by their respective methods, just as an expert abacus operator can move the beads in a mental image of an abacus, or a chess master can play a game of chess blindfolded. Using the circles mentally is, of course, much easier than blindfold chess or abacus operation.

Tautologous or equivalent statements are rendered visually obvious by the circles. For example, we make separate diagrams for the following two assertions:

$$A \lor \sim B$$
$$B \supset A$$

The two diagrams prove to be identical.

Let us now consider a simple three-term problem involving the following premises:

$A \supset B$ (A implies B)
$B \not\equiv C$ (Either B or C but not both)
$A \lor C$ (Either A or C or both)
$C \supset A$ (C implies A)

After shading the circles for the above assertions we are left with the diagram shown in Figure 43. Only one compartment, $AB \sim C$,

NOTATION

- **•** Conjunction ("And")
- **⊃** Implication ("If ___ then ___")
- **v** Disjunction, alternation ("Either ___ or ___ or both")
- **≢** Exclusive disjunction, non-equivalence ("Either ___ or ___ but not both")
- **≡** Equivalence ("If and only if ___ then ___")
- **|** Non-conjunction ("Not both ___ and ___")
- **~** Negation ("Not")

BINARY RELATION	NEGATION
A ⊃ B — If A is true, then B is true	A•~B — A is true and B is false
B ⊃ A — If B is true, then A is true	B•~A — B is true and A is false
A v B — Either A or B is true, or both	~A•~B — Both A and B are false
A ≢ B — Either A or B is true, but not both	A ≡ B — If and only if A is true, B is true
A|B — A and B cannot both be true	A•B — Both A and B are true
A ≡ B — If and only if A is true, B is true	A ≢ B — Either A or B is true, but not both
A•B — Both A and B are true	A|B — A and B cannot both be true

Figure 42.

has not been eliminated. We are forced to conclude, therefore, that, on the basis of the logical structure asserted by the four premises, *A* and *B* must be true and *C* false.

Four-term problems can be solved in the same manner on Venn's four-term figure of intersecting ellipses. Problems with larger numbers of variables are best handled on graphs such as those suggested by Marquand, Carroll, and others, or else one can simply make a list of all the combinations, then cross out the invalid ones. (As we shall see in Chapter 5, this was the method used by Jevons, but of course it is not a diagrammatic one.) After we have

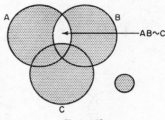

Figure 43.

eliminated all the invalid combinations, an inspection of the remaining ones will give us all that can be validly inferred from the premises. If, for instance, we find that term *D* is true in all the remaining compartments, then *D* must be true. If we find permissible combinations containing both *D* and ∼*D*, we know that *D* is undecided by the premises and may be either true or false. If in performing our eliminations we discover that *all* compartments become shaded, we know that the last diagramed statement introduces a logical contradiction, leading to an absurdity in which nothing can be said about any of the terms. In view of the obvious classroom value of this method of diagraming truth-value problems, it is surprising that most logic textbooks confine their discussion of Venn circles entirely to class logic and the syllogism.

A few remarks should be made about diagraming compound statements with parentheses, such as: $(A \lor B) \supset (B \lor C)$. This asserts that if the relation "*A* ∨ *B*" is a true relation then the relation "*B* ∨ *C*" must also be true.

How can this be shown on the Venn circles? We can of course expand the statement by algebraic methods into a longer statement without parentheses, then make our diagram; but if we do this, we might as well proceed to use algebraic methods throughout. On the other hand, there seems to be no simple way in which the statement, as it stands, can be diagramed. The best procedure is probably to follow the suggestion Peirce made for handling parenthetical statements in class logic—to make separate Venn diagrams for the two relations inside of parentheses, then connect them with another Venn diagram shaded to represent implication.

Figure 44 shows how this appears. The lower set of circles expresses the relation of implication between the binary relations

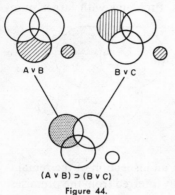

A v B

B v C

(A v B) ⊃ (B v C)

Figure 44.

expressed by the other two sets. This lower set is shaded black because we know the relation to be valid. Gray is used for the other sets of circles because we have no way of knowing whether the relation each expresses is valid or not. If in the course of diagraming other premises we discover that, say, the relation expressed by the upper left circles, "A v B," is valid, we can then blacken the gray area. If, however, we discover that this relation is false, we must convert the relation to its negation. As we have shown earlier, this is done by blacking the white areas and erasing the shading in the other areas.

A knowledge of the truth values of A and B, and in some cases a knowledge of the truth value of one term only, is sufficient to tell us whether the relation A v B is true or false. If, for example, we learn that both terms are false, this clearly contradicts the relation and so we must change it to its negation. If we learn that A is true, this is all we need to know to be sure that the binary relation A v B is true, for it will be true regardless of whether B is true or false. The reader who desires to pursue this further will not find it difficult to work out rules for handling any type of compound statement, including statements that are mixtures of class and propositional assertions. It also is possible to use closed curves and Marquand-type graphs for diagraming certain types of multivalued logics, but if there are more than three terms the diagram or graph becomes so intricate that it ceases to be any sort of visual aid.

The American philosopher Charles Peirce (1839–1914), mentioned several times in this chapter, was deeply interested in logic diagrams. In addition to his extension of Venn's method and an early attempt at what he called an "entitative graph" (later discarded; it was "haunted," Peirce confessed, by "aniconicity"), he finally worked out a comprehensive system by which he believed he could give geometric expression to any conceivable assertion or logical argument. Peirce called it his system of "existential graphs," the term "existential" referring to the graphs' power of depicting any existing state of any aspect of any possible universe. His first attempt to publish a description of the method was in 1897 when he sent an article on the subject to *The Monist* magazine. The editor returned it on the ground that the system could probably be improved. Peirce was so annoyed by this rejection that in a paper written six years later he went out of his way to note that he had not yet found it necessary to make any fundamental alterations in his original scheme. For the rest of his life Peirce regarded the existential graph as his most important contribution to logic; his chef-d'œuvre, he liked to call it. Some idea of how much store Peirce set by this method can be gained from the following quotation:

"Diagrammatic reasoning is the only really fertile reasoning. If logicians would only embrace this method, we should no longer see attempts to base their science on the fragile foundations of metaphysics or a psychology not based on logical theory; and there would soon be such an advance in logic that every science would feel the benefit of it." (*Collected Papers*, Vol. 4, p. 459.)

Again: ". . . if one learns to think of relations in the forms of those graphs, one gets the most distinct and esthetically as well as otherwise intellectually, iconic conception of them likely to suggest circumstances of theoretic utility, that one can obtain in any way. The aid that the system of graphs thus affords to the process of logical analysis, by virtue of its own analytical purity, is surprisingly great, and reaches further than one would dream. Taught to boys and girls before grammar, to the point of thorough familiarization, it would aid them through all their lives. For there are few important questions that the analysis of ideas does not help to answer. The theoretical value of the graphs, too, depends on this." (*Collected Papers*, Vol. 4, p. 516.)

There is not space available in this volume to give a coherent account of Peirce's fantastic diagrammatic method even if I understood it fully, and I am far from assured I do. His several papers on the topic (reprinted in Vol. 4 of his *Collected Papers*) are written in such an elliptic, involuted style that one is led to wonder if Peirce harbored unconscious compulsions toward cloudy writing that would enable him to complain later of his critics' inability to understand him. Add to this opaque style his use of scores of strange terms invented by himself and altered from time to time, and the lack of sufficient drawings to illustrate the meaning of these terms, and the task of comprehending his system becomes formidable indeed.

A few things, however, are clear. Peirce was not attempting to create a method that could be used efficiently for the solution of logic problems, although his graphs could be so used. If one would devote several hours a day for a week or two to practicing with the graphs, Peirce wrote, he would soon be able to solve problems with a facility "about equal" to that of any algebraic method yet devised, including one such system of his own. What Peirce was primarily interested in, however, was a method of analyzing in detail the structure of all deductive reasoning, including mathematical reasoning; breaking the structure into all its elements and giving each element the simplest, most iconic geometrical representation possible. In this way the mind would be able to "see" the logical structure in a fashion analogous to seeing a geographical area when you look at a map. The graphs, he wrote, "put before us moving pictures of thought." They render the structure "literally visible before one's very eyes." In doing this they free the structure from all the "puerilities about words" with which so many English logical works are strewn. "Often not merely strewn with them," he adds, "but buried so deep in them, as by a great snowstorm, as to obstruct the reader's passage and render it fatiguing in the extreme."

In addition to making for clarity, Peirce also believed that, once a formal structure had been adequately graphed, it could then be experimented upon in a manner similar to the way a scientist experiments with a structure in nature. By altering the graph in various ways, adding to it here, taking away there, and so on, one could discover new properties of the structure—properties not previously suspected. In other words, Peirce viewed his graphs in much the same way that Lull viewed his Great Art, as an instrument for the invention and discovery of new truths as well as a device for proving old ones.

Peirce's system is topological throughout. That is to say, his diagrams are unconcerned with size or shape in any metrical sense, but only with such geometrical properties as remain unaltered if the "sheet of assertion" (the piece of paper on which the graphs are drawn) were made of rubber that could be twisted and stretched (or, more precisely, given what topologists call a "continuous deformation"). For example, Peirce made abundant use of closed curves (called "cuts" or "seps") that divide the sheet of assertion into outside and inside regions. The system also relies heavily on "lines of identity," heavy unbroken lines (the shape or length being of no significance) that connect two signs, one at each end of the line. These properties of enclosure and connectivity are of course topological, and in one interesting passage (*Collected Papers*, Vol. 4, p. 346) Peirce says that he expects his system of graphs to contribute toward an understanding of topological laws. On more than one occasion he likens his graphs to chemical diagrams that show how the molecules of a given substance are bonded together in various complex topological structures. The graphs bear an even stronger resemblance, in both appearance and purpose, to the topological figures employed by Kurt Lewin in his *Principles of Topological Psychology*, 1936, and by followers of Lewin who are presently laboring in the field known as "group dynamics."

Peirce sought to make his diagrams as iconic as possible, and in this he partially succeeded. For example: his use of two closed curves, one inside the other (he called this a "scroll"), to indicate what is now called material implication. The outer circle ("outloop") represents the antecedent which, if true, necessitates the truth of all that part of the graph inside the smaller circle ("inloop"). There is also, as Peirce points out, an iconic aspect to his line of identity, as well as its extension into a branching-tree device called a "ligature." But in many other respects (e.g., the use of dotted, wavy, and saw-toothed lines, the use of the underside or "verso" of the sheet as well as other layers of paper beneath to represent other dimensions of possibility, and so on) the iconic aspect is entirely or almost entirely lost. This lack of iconicity is particularly glaring, as Peirce himself confesses, in his later attempt to distinguish within his system the three traditional varieties of modality—factual truth, possible truth, and necessary truth. Peirce did this by the use of three different heraldic "tinctures"—color, fur, and metal—each in turn divided into four types. (The four "colors" are azure, gules, vert, and purpure; the four "furs" are sable, ermine, vair, and potent; the four "metals," argent, or, fer, and plomb.)

58

How Ramon Lull would have been intrigued and utterly mystified by these strange variegated symbols!

These noniconic aspects of Peirce's system give it an air of arbitrariness and disjointedness. The parts do not seem to hang together. One has the feeling that, if twelve competent modern logicians were to set themselves the task of constructing similar graphs that would encompass the whole of logic, each would come up with a different system, and each as good if not better than Peirce's. At any rate, there is no question that Peirce, like Ramon Lull (whom Peirce in an unguarded moment once called an "acute logician"), held a greatly exaggerated notion of the value of his diagrams. That they were an aid to his own thinking is undeniable. He obviously found it desirable to think more in pictures than in words, and after having worked for some twenty years with his own diagrams, he could probably "see" their meanings as effortlessly as an experienced orchestra leader can run his eyes over a musical score and "hear" the orchestration. For the rest of us, however, it would mean a gigantic effort of practice and study to master Peirce's intricate technique to the point of usefulness, and the consensus of logicians who have undergone this initiation is that the system is not worth this effort.[4]

We must remember, however, that Peirce undertook his Gargantuan project at a time when symbolic logic was in its infancy. In many aspects of his method he was a pioneer groping in unfamiliar realms. His logic graphs are still the most ambitious yet attempted, and they are filled with suggestive hints of what can be done along such lines. Peirce himself expected successors to take up where he left off and bring his system to perfection. It would be rash to say that no one in the future will be able to build upon it something closer to what Peirce was striving for. In the meantime, it stands as a characteristic monument to one man's extraordinary industry, brilliance, and eccentricity.

References

1. Venn's criticisms of both Euler's and Lambert's methods are reinforced by Peirce in his *Collected Papers*, Vol. 4, pp. 297 ff. Peirce wrote of course before the development of modern topology, and so his analysis of why Euler's circles do what they do has for modern ears a quaint clumsiness. For a defense and improvement of Lambert's linear method, see the chapter on logic diagrams in John Neville Keynes's *Studies and Exercises in Formal Logic,* fourth edition, 1906. The author was the father of the noted economist John Maynard Keynes.

2. Branko Grünbaum, in "Venn Diagrams and Independent Families of Sets," *Mathematics Magazine,* Vol. 40, January, 1975, pp. 12–23, shows how five identical ellipses can form a Venn diagram and proves that ellipses cannot be used for more than five terms. Convex closed curves will form diagrams for any number of terms, as proved by Vern S. Poythress and Hugo S. Sun in "A Method to Construct Convex Connected Venn Diagrams for Any Finite Number of Sets," *Pentagon,* Spring 1972, pp. 80–83. For any prime number of terms it may be possible to use congruent convex polygons. David W. Henderson reported constructions for 3, 5, and 7 terms in "Venn Diagrams for More Than Four Classes," *American Mathematical Monthly,* Vol. 70, April, 1963, pp. 424–426. For four-term diagrams using congruent rectangles and congruent equilateral triangles, see the answer to Problem 2314, *ibid.,* Vol. 79, October, 1972, pp. 907–908.

On extending Venn diagrams by using nonconvex curves see the 1909 paper by Hocking cited on page 45; Edmund C. Berkeley, "Boolean Algebra," in *Record,* Vol. 26, Part 2, October, 1937, and Vol. 27, Part 1, June, 1938, reprinted as a booklet by Berkeley and Associates, 1952; Trenchard More, Jr., "On the Construction of Venn Diagrams," *Journal of Symbolic Logic,* Vol. 24, December, 1959, pp. 303–304; Margaret E. Baron, "A Note on the Historical Development of Logic Diagrams," *Mathematical Gazette,* Vol. 53, May, 1969, pp. 113–125; Lynette J. Bowles, "Logic Diagrams for Up to *n* Classes," *ibid.,* Vol. 55, December, 1971, pp. 370–373; and S. N. Collings, "Further Logic Diagrams in Various Dimensions," *ibid.,* Vol. 56, December, 1972, pp. 309–310.

An application of Venn diagrams to multivalued logics is given by Solomon W. Golomb in "Connected Logic Diagrams," an unpublished paper, 1966.

3. Walter E. Steurman's "Boole table" combines Macfarlane's chart with Lambert's diagram. See his "Plotting Boolean Functions," *American Mathematical Monthly,* Vol. 67, February, 1960, pp. 170–172, and "The Boole Table Generalized," *ibid.,* Vol. 68, January, 1961, pp. 53–56.

A defect of the Venn and Marquand systems is that after shading a diagram, it is hard to distinguish individual statements. To remedy this, Karl Döhmann proposed diagraming each statement on a separate transparent sheet, using different colors, then superimposing them on the basic diagram. He explained his method in a privately printed booklet, *Eine logistische Farbenquadrat-Methode,* Berlin, 1962.

Closely related to Marquand diagrams is the use of nested crossmarks, with dots to indicate nonempty compartments. See John F. Randolph, "Cross-Examining Propositional Calculus and Set Operations," *American Mathematical Monthly,* Vol. 72, February, 1965, pp. 117–127; and Larry Babcock's contribution to "Scrapbook," in the *Pentagon,* Spring, 1969, pp. 86–88. Compare Margaret Wiscamb's similar approach, "Graphing True-False Statements," *Mathematics Teacher,* Vol. 62, November, 1969, pp. 553–556, and the nested crossmarks used by W. E. Johnson, explained in Venn's *Symbolic Logic,* pp. 326–329.

4. A gallant effort to explain Peirce's graphs has been made by Don Davis Roberts in *The Existential Graphs of Charles S. Peirce,* Mouton, 1973.

3: A Network Diagram for the Propositional Calculus

Venn circles and other diagrams of the shaded-compartment type can, as we have seen in the previous chapter, be used for solving problems in the propositional calculus. In many respects, however, their application to this type of logic is clumsy and lacking in what Peirce called "iconicity"—formal resemblance to the logical structure for which they are intended to be visual aids. This is understandable since these diagrammatic methods were originally devised for class logic. To use them for truth-value problems we have to think of the problems in terms of class logic before the diagram takes on an iconic aspect. Is it possible to diagram statements in the calculus of propositions in such a way that the diagrams exhibit more directly the formal structure of truth-value relations?

In 1951 I set myself the pleasant task of trying to work out such a system. After experimenting with several different approaches I finally hit upon the network method that will form the content of this chapter. It obviously is not intended as a method to compete in efficiency with algebraic or truth-table methods, but it does have, it seems to me, some merit in helping novices such as myself to visualize truth-value structure and to understand better the matrix method of analysis. In addition, it provides a handy means for checking results obtained by other methods. That it can be much improved, I have no doubt. Perhaps it will catch the fancy of some reader who will discover, in toying with the method, some way of eliminating its chief defects and rendering it more elegant.

The most annoying drawback of the Venn circles, when applied to propositional problems, is the difficulty of separating the premises from each other on the diagram so that they can be analyzed separately or altered as desired. This might be done by using sheets of transparent paper (shading each premise on a different sheet) but such a procedure is troublesome, and of course it cannot be applied to classroom blackboards. The network method to be explained here requires only paper and pencil, or chalk and blackboard, and it diagrams a series of premises in such fashion that the structure of each individual premise is visually separate from the others. This makes it possible for the eye to explore any desired portion of the structure in a way that is difficult on diagrams of the Venn type. Essentially, the method is a geometrical analogue of the truth-table or matrix method of handling propositional logic, its iconicity yielding valuable insights into the nature of matrix analysis.

Like all the geometric methods considered so far, this one also is topological, exploiting the "connectivity" properties of linear networks in such manner that the network becomes an isomorph of the logical structure being analyzed. That the propositional calculus can be translated into network theory has been widely recognized for almost two decades, playing an important role in the designing of electric circuits for giant computing machines and, as we shall see in Chapter 8, in the construction of electric logic machines. But so far as I am aware, this is the first attempt at a network analogue simple enough to be serviceable as a blackboard or paper method of solving truth-value problems.

The first step in diagraming a problem is to represent each term by two vertical, parallel lines which stand for the two possible truth values of each term. By convention, the line on the left represents "true," the line on the right "false." If there are, say, five terms involved in a given problem, the basic graph of Figure 45 is drawn.

A simple assertion that a term is true or false is indicated by a cross mark on the appropriate truth-value line, as shown in Figure 46.

Statements expressing a relation between two terms are shown on the graph by one, two, or three horizontal lines that connect a truth-value line of one term with a truth-value line of another.

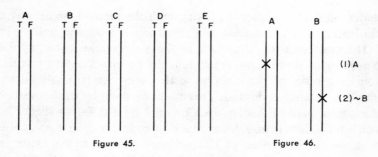

Figure 45.   Figure 46.

These horizontal lines will be called "shuttles." It is necessary to give them some sort of name, and this seems appropriate because in solving a problem, as we shall see, we actually do shuttle back and forth along these lines in much the same manner that Manhattan's 42nd Street shuttle train moves back and forth between the Seventh Avenue and Lexington Avenue subway lines.

It is apparent that only four different kinds of shuttles can be drawn to connect a given pair of terms (Figure 47).

These four shuttles correspond to the four rows of a truth table for two terms. They connect true with true, true with false, false with true, and false with false. If we now wish to show a functional relation between two terms, we have only to eliminate the shuttle or shuttles that represent invalid combinations of truth values. Or put another way, to show only shuttles that indicate permissible combinations.

To illustrate, let us consider first the relation of conjunction ("and"), symbolized by ▪. Only one line of a truth table is valid for this relation; therefore we graph it with a single shuttle, as Figure 48 makes clear.

If the relation of conjunction stands alone as a complete premise (that is, if it is not part of a longer statement), then it states unequivocally the truth value of each term. In such cases we im-

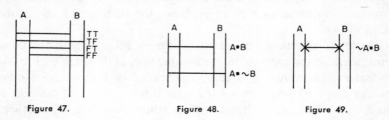

Figure 47.   Figure 48.   Figure 49.

mediately place a cross at each end of the shuttle as shown in Figure 49.

If, however, the conjunction is part of a compound statement, we cannot add the crosses for we have no way of knowing whether the relation itself is true or false. This will be made clear later when we consider the diagraming of compound statements.

The biconditional, or statement of equivalence (symbolized by ≡), requires two shuttles. In ordinary speech this is expressed by saying, "If and only if A is true, then B is true." Its truth table has two valid lines, TT and FF; therefore we diagram it as in Figure 50.

The two shuttles show clearly that, if we are "riding" (to labor the subway metaphor a moment) on A's T line, we have only one shuttle that will carry us to B, and it will land us on B's T line. Similarly, the only available shuttle on A's F line carries us to B's F line. The same relations hold if we move backward from B to A. In other words, if either term is true the other must be true; if either is false, the other must be false.

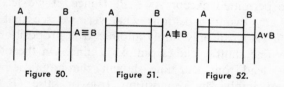

Figure 50.   Figure 51.   Figure 52.

The exclusive "or" of nonequivalence (symbolized by ≢) likewise is expressed by two shuttles (Figure 51).

The diagram shows at a glance that if one term is true the other must be false, and vice versa. A comparison of this pattern with the previous one reveals an interesting fact. Each diagram is made up of the shuttles *missing* from the other. This tells us that one is the negation of the other. Just as we transformed a Venn diagram of a binary relation into its negation by exchanging the black and white areas, so we can in this method effect the same transformation simply by erasing whatever shuttles are present and substituting those that are absent.

The inclusive "or" of disjunction ("either or both"), symbolized by v, requires three shuttles. Inspection of Figure 52 will show that it is the negation of ∼ A ∎ ∼ B.

The statement "not both A and B are true" (sometimes referred to as the Sheffer stroke function), will be symbolized by A | B.

It is the negation of $A \cdot B$, and likewise requires three shuttles (Figure 53).

The "If . . . then" of a conditional statement, symbolized by $\supset$, also calls for three shuttles.[1] Unlike the previous relations, it is not symmetrical. That is, the diagram has two forms, depending on which term implies the other. These two forms are indicated in Figure 54.

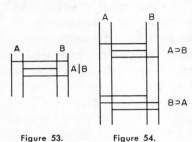

Figure 53.   Figure 54.

The shuttles reveal immediately that $A \supset B$ is the negation of $A \cdot \sim B$, and $B \supset A$ is the negation of $\sim A \cdot B$. The diagrams are excellent classroom devices for explaining the so-called paradoxes of material implication. The statement "A implies B" has no meaning in the propositional calculus other than what is indicated by the shuttles in its diagram; namely, that all combinations of truth values are permitted except $A \cdot \sim B$. Hence, if we let A and B stand for any two propositions whatever, we see that any true proposition (A) can only imply another true proposition (B) because only one shuttle leads from A's T line. On the other hand, two shuttles lead from A's F line, showing that any false proposition ($\sim A$) may imply any proposition, true or false (B or $\sim B$). Similarly, the two shuttles leading from B's T line tell us that any true proposition (B) may be implied by any proposition, true or false (A or $\sim A$), whereas the single shuttle terminating on B's F line indicates that a false proposition ($\sim B$) can be implied only by another false proposition ($\sim A$). The paradoxical character of such assertions as, "If grass is red then Shakespeare wrote *Hamlet*," vanishes as soon as we realize that the "if . . . then" of material implication has a different meaning in the calculus than in common speech. It is not intended to assert any causal connection between the two propositions, but only to tell us what combinations of true and false values are permitted by the relation.

We have now covered all the binary functions for which there are common expressions in the language and commonly used symbols in logic. It should be clear that any statement of a truth-value relation between two terms can easily be diagramed. The relations discussed occur so often, however, that one's use of the graph will be greatly facilitated if they are committed to memory so that it will not be necessary to pause and analyze the relation, or to refer to a chart of their shuttle patterns each time a relation has to be graphed. The order in which the shuttles for a given relation are drawn is not, of course, significant. But if they are memorized as patterns, it will be convenient to adopt a specific order of shuttles for each relation. The order adopted here is one that conforms to the most commonly used order of combinations in truth-table lines.

When one or both terms of a binary relation are negative, as, for example, $\sim A \vee B$, how do we go about drawing the required shuttles? The procedure is simple. We consider the pattern for $A \vee B$, then exchange the terminal points of A's two truth-value lines. In other words, all shuttles on A's T line are shifted to the F line; all shuttles on A's F line are shifted to the T line. The terminal points on B remain unchanged. After we have done this we shall discover that the resulting diagram is identical with the diagram for $A \supset B$. The same pattern also results if we diagram $\sim B \supset \sim A$ (in this case we must of course exchange the terminal points on the truth-value lines of *both* terms). Whenever the diagrams for two assertions are identical, then they are said to be "tautologies," that is, merely two ways of saying the same thing. We can express the identity of $\sim A \vee B$ and $A \supset B$ by connecting them with the symbol of equivalence: $\sim A \vee B \equiv A \supset B$. Such a statement is called an "equivalence formula." Diagrammatically, the equivalence of two binary relations is revealed by the fact that they have identical shuttle patterns.

Additional examples will make this clear. De Morgan called attention to two interesting tautologies known as "De Morgan's laws." One tells us that the denial of a conjunction can be expressed by denying each term separately in a disjunctive relation. Symbolically, this is the equivalence formula, $A \mid B \equiv \sim A \vee \sim B$. The other law tells us that the denial of a disjunction can be expressed by denying both terms of a conjunctive relation: $\sim (A \vee B) \equiv \sim A \bullet \sim B$. We can establish both laws simply by diagraming the two sides of their formula. If the diagrams are identical, then the two statements are tautological.

Before going into the matter of diagraming chains of terms connected by the same relation, or compound statements involving parentheses, let us consider the actual graphing and solution of two simple problems.

For our first problem, we are given the following four premises:

1. If A is true then B is true. $(A \supset B)$
2. Either B is true or C is true, but not both. $(B \not\equiv C)$
3. Either A is true or C is true, or both. $(A \vee C)$
4. B is true. (B)

What can we infer about A and C?

Our first step is to diagram the premises. When this is done, our graph will appear as shown in Figure 55.

The next step is to examine the network structure to see if it will unequivocally determine the truth values of A and C. Since we know the value of B, we begin our exploration at the cross mark on B's T line. We run our eyes upward along this line to see if we encounter a premise in which there is a *single* shuttle terminating on the line. In this case we find such a shuttle in premise 2. Since this shuttle indicates a permissible line of travel, and since the premise does not offer us a choice of more than one shuttle, we are obliged to follow the single shuttle to its terminal point on C's F line. Our passage on this shuttle is indicated by placing cross marks at the two terminal points of the shuttle. The cross mark on C's F line tells us that premise 2, in combination with premise 4, forces us to conclude that C is false. We next inspect C's F line and we quickly discover that in premise 3 we come upon a single shuttle terminating on this line. We make a cross mark at this point, follow the shuttle to A's T line, and make a cross mark there also.

We have now determined that C is false and A is true, but we must continue our examination of the network to make certain that the premises do not contain a contradiction. Inspection of A's T line reveals a single shuttle in premise 1. We mark the terminal point with a cross, follow the shuttle to B's T line, and mark its terminal point there. This last cross mark is consistent with our previous knowledge that B is true. Since there are no other single shuttles terminating on the truth-value lines that bear cross marks, we conclude that the premises are consistent, and consistent only with the truth of A and B, and falsity of C. If the premises had contained a contradiction, it would have forced us, in our exploration

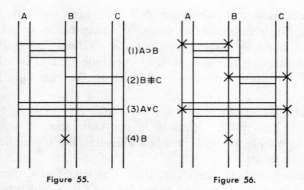

Figure 55.   Figure 56.

of the structure, to affirm both the truth and falsity of at least one term, and possibly all terms.

Figure 56 shows how the graph appears after our problem has been solved.

Let us now consider a slightly more difficult problem—one in which we are not told the truth value of any term. Our premises are:

1. In August I either wear a hat or go bareheaded.
2. I never go bareheaded in August when I have on a bow tie.
3. In August I either wear a hat or a bow tie and sometimes both.

To put these statements into symbolic form, we assign the following meanings to A, B, and C.

A—I wear a hat in August.
B—I wear a bow tie in August.
C—I go bareheaded in August.

The premises can now be stated symbolically as:

1. $A \not\equiv C$
2. $B \mid C$
3. $A \lor B$

A network diagram of the premises will show the structure of Figure 57.

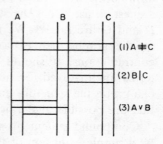

(1) $A \not\equiv C$
(2) $B \mid C$
(3) $A \lor B$

Figure 57.

We must now test this structure to see what we can discover about the truth values of its terms. We may begin anywhere; so suppose we start by making a cross on A's T line. The single shuttle in the first premise forces us to conclude that C is false, but this is as far as our exploration will take us. We can learn nothing about B.

The next step is to erase all cross marks and place a cross on A's F line. This quickly leads us to contradictions. If we explore the structure fully we find ourselves affirming the truth and falsity of all three terms.

We must conclude, therefore, that A is true and C false. One final step remains. B must be tested for both true and false values to see if contradictions arise. No such contradictions are encountered, telling us that the truth of A and the falsity of C are consistent with either value for B. Hence the answer to our problem is that in August I always wear a hat, never go bareheaded, but may or may not sport a bow tie.

In some cases the test of one term is sufficient to establish the truth values of all terms. In other problems, as in the foregoing, a test of one term will give values for only a portion of the remaining terms. Further tests then have to be made to see if the undetermined terms are capable of determination by the structure, or whether the structure leaves a certain number of terms undecidable. It may be, of course, that a given structure will leave all terms undecidable. Or it may be that certain premises are contradictory. In any case, the graph gives a clear visual picture of the structure that is open for inspection and experimentation in a way that is often difficult and confusing if one is using truth-table procedures. For example, if we have a structure that does not determine the truth value of any term, we may wish to answer such a question as, "Does the structure permit A and F to be true when D and G are false?" We have only to make these four assertions on the graph, then explore the structure to see if they lead to contradictions. It should be clear that, regardless of how many terms are involved, or how many binary relations are given, we can graph the structure and perform upon it any of the operations that are possible algebraically.

Compound statements involving parentheses can be diagrammed by a simple extension of the graph. We shall illustrate this by considering the assertion $(A \vee B) \supset (C \vee D)$. The two disjunctive statements inside parentheses are first diagramed in the usual manner, as if they were two premises, except that dotted lines are used for shuttles instead of solid lines. (This corresponds to the use of gray shading when Venn circles are used for compound statements.) The dotted lines indicate the tentative nature of the shuttles; that is, we do not as yet know whether the relation they symbolize is a true or false one. If we later learn that it is true, we change the dotted lines to solid. If we learn that it is false, we leave the dotted lines (or erase them if we wish) and add in solid lines the *negation* of the original pattern. As explained earlier, this is done by supplying in solid lines the shuttles *missing* from the dotted pattern. In either case, if the final result is a *single* shuttle, we immediately place crosses on its terminal points to affirm the truth-value lines that are involved.

The two parenthetical statements must now be connected on the graph by a relation of implication. To do this, we adopt the following procedure. At the right of the graph we draw two pairs of *horizontal* truth-value lines, each pair opposite one of the statements already graphed. By convention we assume the lower line of each pair to be true, the upper line false. If we give the paper a quarter turn clockwise, these truth-value lines will appear as a familiar graph for two terms, except in this case each term is itself a binary relation. On this graph we place the shuttle lines of implication to show that one relation implies the other. These shuttles are solid lines since there is no uncertainty about their validity. The entire graph will now appear like Figure 58.

If a single term is involved in a compound statement, for example, $A \vee (B \cdot C)$, the same procedure is adopted. In such a case we show the tentative character of A by using a half cross or diagonal mark. It is easily changed to true by adding the other half, or negated by placing a cross mark on A's F line. The graph for the entire expression will appear as in Figure 59.

A chain of terms connected by the same relation can often be diagramed by one or more shuttles with small circles at required spots along each shuttle to mark the truth-value lines that are involved. For example, $A \cdot \sim B \cdot D$ can be graphed in the manner of Figure 60.

If the chain stands alone as a complete premise, we can of course

70

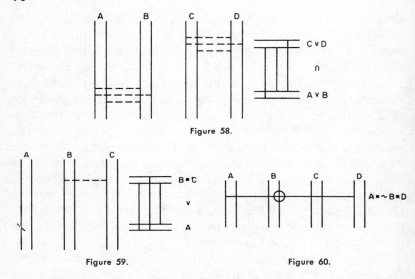

Figure 58.

Figure 59.   Figure 60.

place X's on each truth-value line involved in the chain. If part of a compound statement, however, the shuttle must be dotted and the X's cannot be added until we discover that the entire chain is a valid relation. The intersection point surrounded by the small circle is treated exactly as if it were the terminal point of a shuttle. The absence of a circle on either of C's truth-value lines indicates that C is not involved in the chain.

A chain of equivalent relations, such as $A \equiv B \equiv C$, can be diagrammed as in Figure 61, with two shuttles, using small circles on B's truth-value lines.

Similar procedures can be worked out for statements that tell us only one term in a series is true, or that all the terms cannot be false, or that any combination of truth values is permitted except all true and all false, and so on. In such cases, of course, we are merely showing the valid lines of a truth table for the entire chain of terms. In the above three-term example, we make use of two valid lines of an eight-line table. Consequently, if we found it necessary to negate the chain we would have to replace the two shuttles by the six missing ones.

When there are more than three terms in a chain, the number of shuttles involved may become too troublesome to handle and we may find it simpler to break the chain into parenthetical phrases and diagram them by extending the graph to the right as previously explained. For example, if we interpret the chain $A \vee B \vee C \vee D$ to mean that all the terms cannot be false, we can diagram this as $(A \vee B) \vee (C \vee D)$.

Conversely, we may sometimes find it convenient to take a compound expression such as $A \supset (B \cdot C)$, and instead of diagraming it by extending the graph, we can work out an eight-line truth table for the entire expression and picture it as shown in Figure 62.

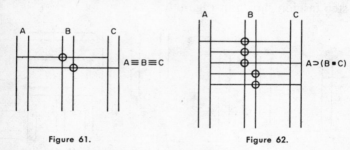

Figure 61.   Figure 62.

This is a diagrammatic way of expanding the original statement to what logicians call its "normal disjunctive" form. Each shuttle in the above diagram represents a valid line of the eight-line truth table. The entire pattern corresponds to the expression $(A \cdot B \cdot C) \vee (\sim A \cdot B \cdot C) \vee (\sim A \cdot B \cdot \sim C) \vee (\sim A \cdot \sim B \cdot C) \vee (\sim A \cdot \sim B \cdot \sim C)$.

When the same terms appear more than once in a statement it often is possible to reduce the statement to a simpler form before diagraming it. For example, the statement $(A \cdot \sim B) \vee (\sim A \cdot \sim B)$ can be diagramed as parenthetical statements connected by the inclusive "or" relation. But since we are dealing with only two terms, and since shuttles belonging to the same binary relation represent disjunctive possibilities, it is much simpler to diagram the statement as in Figure 63.

This is still not the simplest diagram, for we see at once that, regardless of the truth or falsity of A, B must be false, whereas knowing B to be false tells us nothing about A. Consequently, we can picture the original assertion simply by making a cross on B's F line (Figure 64).

In other words, the formula $(A \cdot \sim B) \vee (\sim A \cdot \sim B) \equiv \sim B$ is a tautology. Thus we see how the network graph can be used

as a visual aid in the task of reducing a statement to its most economical or "logically powerful" form. There are a number of rules
that can be followed for the elimination of unnecessary shuttles and
other steps involved in the "minimizing" of a statement, but the
subject is too complicated to go into here.

For long statements containing parentheses within parentheses,
the graph may be extended as far as we please by adding additional
truth-value lines, alternating horizontal with vertical graphs in the
stair-step fashion shown in Figure 65.

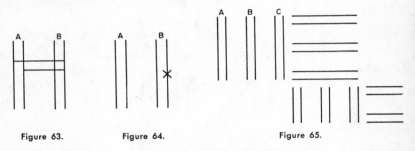

Figure 63.   Figure 64.   Figure 65.

This stair-step procedure will obviously take care of as many
parenthetical levels as desired. All patterns must of course be
shown as tentative (half crosses and dotted shuttles) except for
the final relation shown in the lower right corner. This relation
alone is not tentative and therefore is expressed by solid shuttles.

We cannot go into all the details involved in solving problems
expressed by compound statements, but the reader who is sufficiently interested will not find it difficult to work out his own
rules. The following important rules should make clear the general
nature of the procedure.

1. If the truth values of all individual terms within a parenthetical statement are known, and they conform to one of the
dotted shuttles for that statement, then the entire statement is
known to be true.

In some cases, knowing the truth value of one term only is
sufficient to establish the truth value of the entire function. In
the relation of implication, for example, the falsity of A is all the
information we need to know that $A \supset B$ is a true function because
there are two shuttles leading from A's F line. In other words,
there is a shuttle for FT and another for $FF;$ so regardless of

whether B is true or false, there will be a shuttle to represent the combination. In similar fashion the truth of B is sufficient to tell us that $A \supset B$ must be true. We encounter similar situations with $A \mid B$ and $A \lor B$. We can phrase the procedure as follows. When we know the truth value of one term only, and there are two shuttles leading from this truth-value line, we can then affirm the truth of the entire binary function. If there is only one shuttle, we lack sufficient information to do this.

2. If the terms are known to have a combination of truth values *not* indicated by a shuttle, the entire relation is known to be false.

3. Whenever a parenthetical statement is known to be true, either because of knowledge of its terms or because it is found to be true in the process of exploring the entire structure, its shuttles are changed to solid lines or its half crosses to crosses. The truth of the entire statement is then indicated by a cross mark on the T line in the pair of truth-value lines (to the right or below) that correspond to the statement.

4. Whenever a parenthetical statement is known to be false, in either of the two ways mentioned above, we add the missing shuttle or shuttles in solid lines. The falsity of the entire relation is then indicated by a cross mark on the F line in the pair of truth-value lines that correspond to the statement.

Let us illustrate the entire procedure with an elementary problem of a type not hitherto considered. Suppose we wish to know whether the statement $(A \supset B) \supset (B \supset A)$ is a valid theorem. If it is, then it must hold for all possible value combinations of A and B. To determine this we first diagram the statement as in Figure 66.

We must now test this structure for the four possible combinations of values for A and B—a diagrammatic procedure corresponding to the matrix method of testing a theorem. If none of these combinations produces a contradiction, we know the structure represents a valid logical law. Our testing procedure will show that the combinations $TT, TF,$ and FF are all consistent, but when we test for FT we encounter a contradiction. Let us see how this occurs.

The first step in testing for FT is to make a cross on A's F line and a cross on B's T line as shown in the illustration below. Since this combination is represented by a shuttle in the pattern for the lower statement, we know that the lower statement is true. Consequently, we change its dotted shuttles to solid ones and indicate the truth of the relation by a cross on the corresponding T line on the right. Since there is but one shuttle attached to this line, we must follow the shuttle to the T line of the upper pair of horizontal truth-value lines. This tells us that the upper statement, $B \supset A$, is also true. We indicate this by putting a cross on its T line and changing its shuttles to solid lines. The graph should now look like Figure 67.

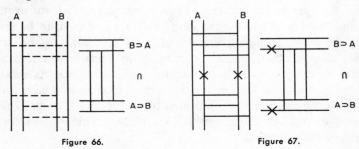

Figure 66.   Figure 67.

We are obviously involved in a contradiction. For if we explore A's F line, affirmed with a cross mark, we encounter a single shuttle that carries us to B's F line. But this contradicts our assumption that B is true. Similarly, the single shuttle attached to B's T line will carry us to A's T line, contradicting our assumption that A is false.

Examination of the structure could have proceeded in other ways, but the results would have been the same. For example, we might have begun by finding the upper relation false, in which case the vertical shuttles on the right would have forced us to conclude that the lower relation was also false. Knowing it to be false, we supply in a solid line the missing shuttle. This in turn tells us that A is true and B false, thus contradicting our original assumptions about A and B. Of course it does not matter in the least how we go about exploring the structure. As soon as we encounter a contradiction, we know that the statement we are testing is not a law. If we do not come upon a contradiction, as, for example, in testing $(A \supset B) \lor (B \supset A)$, then we know it is a valid theorem.

Syllogisms can be tested in this way to determine if they are laws, but the process is awkward, especially if particular statements are involved. To give one example, suppose we wished to test the validity of the syllogism:

> All A is B
> No B is C
> Therefore, no A is C

This can be stated in the propositional calculus as the following theorem: $[(A \supset B) \blacksquare B \mid C] \supset A \mid C$. When we test it for the eight possible combinations of values for the three terms, it proves to be valid in all cases. A particular statement, such as "Some A is B," must be handled as a disjunction—in this case, $(A \blacksquare B \blacksquare C)$ v $(A \blacksquare B \blacksquare \sim C)$.

It should be unnecessary to point out that all the rules given in this chapter for the manipulation of network diagrams apply only to a material interpretation of implication. They do not apply to a system of "strict implication" such as proposed by Clarence I. Lewis, in which the consequent of an implication must be formally deducible from the antecedent. In strict implication, knowing the truth values of individual terms in a conditional relation is not sufficient to tell you the truth value of the entire statement except when the antecedent is known to be true and the consequent false (in which case the implication is known to be false). I suspect that the network method can, with the adoption of suitable conventions, be adapted to strict implication logics, but this is a use for the method that is beyond my capacities to explore.

It is also possible, I think, to combine this system with the Venn circles so that problems involving a mixture of class-inclusion statements and truth-value statements can be handled together. Still another interesting possibility is that of extending the network method to take care of multivalued logics that are based on truth-table matrices.[2] For example, a three-value logic could be diagramed by increasing the number of truth-value lines under each term from two to three. Since shuttles in such a logic represent two types of relations, true and "indeterminate" (or whatever one wishes to call the third value), it will be necessary to distinguish two types of shuttle lines. This could be done by making "true" shuttles solid and using a saw-toothed line for the new value.

Exactly what pattern of shuttles to use for a given function will depend on the type of three-value logic we are considering. Here we enter the realm of Lewis Carroll's Humpty Dumpty, for whom words meant just what he wanted them to mean. In multivalued logics, connectives such as "and" and "implies" cease to have intuitive meanings and are used merely to express a specific matrix pattern of values. To make this a bit clearer, let us reflect a moment on the meaning of "and" in two-value logic. The assertion "*A* and *B* are true" can be diagramed with two cross marks or a single shuttle as shown in Figure 68.

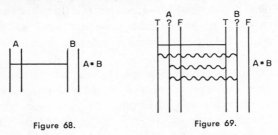

Figure 68.   Figure 69.

This shuttle tells us that the other three possible shuttles represent nonpermissible or "false" combinations of values for *A* and *B;* hence they are eliminated from the diagram. In three-value logic the situation is not so simple. In the first place we have nine possible shuttles for every pair of terms. We know that the statement "*A* and *B*" requires a solid shuttle from *A*'s *T* line to *B*'s *T* line, but how are we to interpret the other eight combinations of values? The answer is that we can interpret them any way we choose, basing our decision on such factors as an analogy with two-value logic, a pleasing symmetry or richness in the pattern, some intended meaning for the third value, and so on. Each interpretation of "and" will involve us in a different brand of three-value logic. Jan Lukasiewicz, Emil Post, and Barkley Rosser have a preference for an "and" that can be represented by the shuttle pattern of Figure 69.

On the other hand, the Russian logician D. A. Bochvar based an interesting three-valued logic on the pattern of Figure 70.

Like the paradoxes of material implication, a great many mysteries of three-value logics are cleared up when we realize that words like "and," "not," and "implies" have only the most tenuous analogy, if any at all, with their meanings in everyday speech. A three-value logic function means nothing more than the particular matrix pattern (in our case, the shuttle pattern) that is permitted by that relation. If instead of saying "*A* implies *B*" in a three-value system we said "*A* galumphs *B*," considerable clarity might result.

Figure 71 shows how the shuttles for "*A* implies *B*" appear when we diagram the relation in the three-value system proposed by Lukasiewicz and Alfred Tarski.

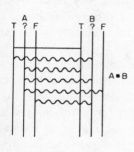

Figure 70.

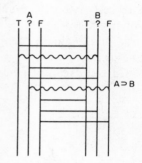

Figure 71.

There is as little to be gained in trying to understand the "meaning" of this relation as in trying to visualize a four-dimensional cube. The pattern itself is all the meaning the relation need have. It is interesting to note that if we remove all the shuttles that have terminal points on a ? line we are left with the familiar shuttle pattern of two-value implication. There is a sense, therefore, in which the two-value structure is a subsystem of this larger matrix.

Many-valued logics of more than three values, such as Hans Reichenbach's probability logic, would require additional truth-value lines, one for each value in the system. The different types of shuttles could be distinguished by using different colored pencils (corresponding colors could also be used for the value lines). I do not think the difficulties here are insuperable, but perhaps the complexity of rules that would be necessary for manipulating such graphs would make them too unwieldy to be useful.

Even in the humdrum world of two-value logic it is sometimes expedient to graph a problem with value lines that stand for something other than true and false. Suppose we are told that Smith, Jones, and Robinson are professors of physics, mathematics, and philosophy, though not necessarily respectively. A group of premises tells us that, if Jones teaches physics, Robinson teaches mathematics, and so on. One approach to this familiar type of brain teaser would be to make a graph for nine propositions (Smith is a philosophy professor, Smith is a physics professor, etc.), each capable of being true or false. However, since the three faculty posts are taken as mutually exclusive, a simpler approach is to use only three terms (standing for the three men), each with three value lines to represent the three subjects which they teach. In a way, this is solving the problem by a kind of three-value logic, though not a true multivalue system since the relations still must be either true or false.

Lewis Carroll's plan of placing counters on a graph can also be adapted to the network system. Instead of truth-value lines we have truth-value columns in which counters may be placed to indicate permissible true and false combinations. A sheet of graph paper can be used as the "board," and buttons or beans can serve as counters. The statement $(A \supset B) \lor (B \equiv C)$ would appear on the board as shown in Figure 72.

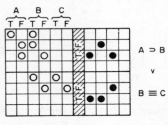

Figure 72.

To indicate the tentative nature of the relations inside parentheses we use counters of a different color from those used for the nontentative relation on the right of the graph. Counters that are one color on one side, another color on the other, would be convenient because then, if we wished to change a relation from tentative to true, we would only have to turn over its counters. Obviously, all rules that apply to the network method can be adapted to the counter method. Although this procedure is in some ways less iconic with propositional logic than the other, in other ways it more closely resembles the matrix method of truth tables. It has the advantage of making it easy to alter the structure in any desired way without the annoyance of having to erase. If one wishes to simplify a structure by eliminating unnecessary shuttles, then it has a decided advantage. Actually, this counter method is really a primitive abacus for performing logic operations; it is as much a "logic machine" as a "diagram."

As we shall see in the chapters to follow, most of the logic machines that have so far been constructed, from Lord Stanhope's syllogism device to modern electrical machines for the propositional calculus, operate by principles that are intimately related to the diagrammatic procedures sketched in this and the preceding chapter.

References

1. All binary functions involving three shuttles can be reduced to two "one-way" shuttles by using arrows to indicate that travel is in one direction only. Thus $A \supset B$ could be shown as:

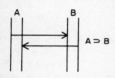

In some cases, this is an efficient type of diagram to use, but it was not introduced in the chapter because it unduly complicates the system and also because it reduces the system's iconicity. In the construction of electrical machines, however, these "one-way" shuttles (circuits made one-way by relays or electronic devices) play an important role.

2. Concerning multivalued logics, the only intelligible popular account known to me is by J. Barkley Rosser, "On the Many-valued Logics," *American Journal of Physics*, Vol. 9, August, 1941, p. 207. For more advanced discussions see Emil Post's classic paper, "Introduction to a General Theory of Elementary Propositions," *American Journal of Mathematics*, Vol. 43, 1921, p. 163; *Symbolic Logic*, by C. I. Lewis and C. H. Langford, 1932; and *Many-valued Logics*, by Rosser and A. R. Turquette, 1952. The latter work contains an excellent selected bibliography. More recent references include *An Introduction to Many-valued Logics*, by Robert Ackermann, 1967, and *Many-valued Logic*, by Nicholas Rescher, 1969.

4: The Stanhope
Demonstrator

Although Ramon Lull made use of rotating disks to facilitate the working of his eccentric system of reasoning, his devices are not "logic machines" in the sense that they can be used for solving problems in formal logic. The inventor of the world's first logic machine, in this stricter sense of the term, was a colorful eighteenth century British statesman and scientist, Charles Stanhope, third Earl Stanhope (1753–1816). His curious device, which he called a "demonstrator," is interesting in more ways than one. Not only could it be used for solving traditional syllogisms by a method closely linked to the Venn circles; it also took care of numerical syllogisms (anticipating De Morgan's analysis of such forms) as well as elementary problems of probability. In addition, it was based on a system of logical notation which clearly fore-shadowed Hamilton's technique of reducing syllogisms to state-ments of identity by making use of negative terms and quantified predicates.

Stanhope's speculations on logic covered a period of some thirty years, but he published nothing about his logical views beyond printing on his own hand press several early chapters of an un-finished work titled *The Science of Reasoning Clearly Explained upon New Principles.* These chapters were circulated only among a few acquaintances. In a letter written shortly before his death he advises a friend not to discuss his logical methods with others lest "some bastard imitation" of his views appear before the publication of his projected work. It was not until sixty years later that one of the earl's contrivances, together with relevant letters and notes, came into the hands of Rev. Robert Harley, who then published an account of the demonstrator and the logic on which it was based. It is from Harley's article, "The Stanhope Demonstrator," *Mind,* Vol. 4, April, 1879, that most of the following account of Lord Stanhope and his unusual device is drawn.

In his day, Stanhope was better known throughout England for his fiery political opinions and confused domestic affairs than for his many scientific inventions. His first wife was the sister of England's young and controversial prime minister, William Pitt.[1] For a time the earl was a supporter of Pitt, but he later broke with the ministry to become a vigorous opponent of most of its measures. As a member of the Revolution Society, formed to honor the Revolution of 1688, his political views were strongly liberal and democratic. His impetuous proposals in the House of Lords were so often and so soundly defeated that he was widely known as the "minority of one," and his thin figure was prominent in the political cartoons of the period. He was an ardent supporter of the French republicans in the early days of the French Revolution. It is said that he even went so far as to discard all the external trappings of his peerage.

At the early age of nineteen he was elected a fellow of the Royal Society and for the rest of his life he devoted a large segment of his time and income to scientific pursuits. His best known inventions were the Stanhope microscopic lens, the Stanhope hand printing press, a monochord for tuning musical instruments, a system for fireproofing buildings, certain improvements in canal locks, a method of stereotyping, and a primitive steamboat. In a book titled *Principles of Electricity,* 1779, he outlines a novel electrical theory of his own. In addition to his logic machine, he also devised an arithmetical calculating machine employing geared wheels.[2]

Before explaining Stanhope's logic demonstrator, it will be necessary first to glance briefly at his logic. It rests on the assumption, later emphasized by George Bentham, William Hamilton, and others, that any proposition in class logic can be interpreted as a statement of identity.[3] Thus if we say "All men are mortal," we can take this to mean that the class of all men is identical to a portion of the class of all mortal things. If we say "Socrates is mortal," we mean that this one man, Socrates, is identical to one of the members of the class of all mortal things. Negative propositions are reduced to identities by changing them to affirmative statements and employing negative terms. For example, "No swans are green" tells us that the class of all swans is identical with a portion of the class of all not-green things.

The following table shows how the four traditional propositions, A,E,I,O, can be rephrased as statements of identity:

A.	All *A* is *B*	All A = Some B
E.	No *A* is *B*	All A = Some not-*B*
I.	Some *A* is *B*	Some A = Some B
O.	Some *A* is not *B*	Some A = Some not-*B*

Stanhope used the term *"holos"* (the Greek word for "whole") to stand for the middle term of a syllogism, choosing this word to underscore the fact that the middle term must be universally distributed in at least one premise before it can successfully mediate an inference concerning the other two terms. The other terms are called *"ho"* and *"los"* (*ho* if it is in the first premise, *los* if in the second. The order of premises is immaterial. The first premise is simply the statement first considered).

"The reader will observe," Stanhope writes, "that *ho* as well as *los* may be identic with *holos,* but that neither *ho* nor *los* can ever exceed *holos*."

In Stanhope's terminology, the demonstrator is simply a device for determining what relation of *ho* to *los* can be deduced by relating each term to the *holos*. The contrivance consists of a block of mahogany 4 inches wide, 4½ inches tall, and ¾ inch thick, with a brass plate mounted on the face (Figure 73). In the center

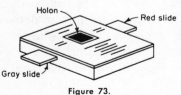

Figure 73.

of the plate is a square window or depression about an inch wide and a half-inch deep. Stanhope calls this window the "holon." It represents "all" of the *holos,* or middle term of whatever syllogism is being examined.

A panel of gray wood stands for the *ho*—the term in the first premise that is not the middle term. It can be pushed into the demonstrator through a slot on the left until it covers part or all of the holon. The *los* (the term in the second premise that is not the middle term) is represented by a panel of transparent red glass that is pushed into the machine through a slot on the right, sliding on top of the gray in case the two slides overlap. Unlike the gray panel, however, it cannot be withdrawn completely from the instrument. As we shall see later, the gray panel can be removed from its slot and inserted through another slot above the holon for working problems in what Stanhope calls the "logic of probability."

A scale from 0 to 10 appears on the brass frame above and to the left of the holon. The same scale also is found on the lower edge of the red slide. Figure 74 shows the face of the demonstrator

DEMONSTRATOR,
INVENTED BY
CHARLES EARL STANHOPE.

The right-hand edge of the gray points out, on this upper scale,
the extent of the gray, in the logic of certainty.

The lower edge of the gray points out, on this side scale, the extent of the gray, in the logic of probability.

The area of the square opening, within the black frame, represents the holon, in all cases.

The right-hand side of the square opening points out, on this lower scale, the extent of the red, in all cases.

The right-hand edge of the gray points out, on the same lower scale, the extent of the consequence, (or dark red,) if any, in the logic of certainty.

Rule for the Logic of Certainty.
To the gray, add the red, and deduct the holon: the remainder, (or dark red,) if any, will be the extent of the consequence.

Rule for the Logic of Probability.
The proportion, between the area of the dark red and the area of the holon, is the probability which results from the gray and the red.

PRINTED BY EARL STANHOPE, CHEVENING, KENT.

Figure 74. Reproduction of the face of Lord Stanhope's demonstrator. (From *Mind*, April, 1879.)

as it appears when both slides are pushed in as far as they will go, the red above the gray and both covering the entire holon.

The working of the device is quite simple. Suppose, for example, we have the following premises:

> No M is A
> All B is M

The first step is to convert these premises into affirmative statements of identity, all the terms properly quantified:

> All M is some not-A
> All B is some M

We insert the gray panel (which stands for "some not-A") into the demonstrator, pushing it to the right until it covers "all" of the holon (which represents M). In other words, "some not-A" is made identical with all of M.

The next step is to push the red slide (all B) until it only partially covers the holon, since all of B is identical with only part of M. Whenever the two slides are forced to overlap, as in this example, the gray panel is visible through the red and we can conclude that an identity has been established between the *ho* and the *los*. In this case we conclude that "all B" is identical with "some not-A." This is the same as saying "No B is A" (or "No A is B"), the traditional valid conclusion of the syllogism. The device, it should be noted, does not show the "weak" conclusions—"Some B is not A" and "Some A is not B." These have to be obtained by immediate inference from "No B is A."

The rules for operating the demonstrator can be summarized as follows:

1. When a premise relates a term to "all" of the middle term, we push the panel for that term over the entire holon.

2. When a premise relates a term to "some" of the middle term, we push the panel for that term over part of the holon.

3. When a premise relates a term to "none" of the middle term (e.g., "No A is M," or in affirmative form, "All A is not-M"), we withdraw the panel for that term so that no part of the holon is covered by it.

4. After the two slides are properly adjusted to represent the two premises, we inspect the holon to see if the slides must of necessity overlap. If so, we may then conclude an identity has been

established between the terms represented by the slides. If the slides are not forced to overlap, no identity is established and therefore no conclusion can be drawn.

A few more examples will make the process clearer.

> No *M* is *A*
> No *M* is *B*

In affirmative form this is:

> All *M* is some not-*A*
> All *M* is some not-*B*

The two slides, standing for "some not-*A*" and "some not-*B*" are each pushed over the entire holon. They must overlap; so we conclude that "Some not-*A* is some not-*B*." This is not, of course, a traditional conclusion, for we have committed the fallacy of beginning with two negative premises and so cannot draw a conclusion about the relation of *A* to *B*. Nevertheless, it is a valid conclusion (assuming that the middle term has members), as can be seen easily by making a Venn diagram of the syllogism. We may even go a step further, Stanhope points out, and conclude that as many not-*A*'s are not-*B*'s as there are *M*'s.

In one case only, that of the traditionally troublesome syllogism *Baroco*, the holon must be regarded as "not-*M*" instead of *M*. The two premises of *Baroco:*

> All *A* is *M*
> Some *B* is not *M*

must be converted to:

> All not-*M* is some not-*A*
> Some *B* is some not-*M*

The gray slide (some not-*A*) is pushed over the entire holon, which in this case represents "not-*M*." The red slide (some *B*) is pushed over part of the holon. The two must overlap, indicating the traditional conclusion of *Baroco*, "Some *B* is some not-*A*," or as commonly expressed, "Some *B* is not *A*."

In such fashion the device can be used to demonstrate valid conclusions from two premises or to show that no valid conclusion can be drawn. The task, however, of translating the premises into proper form is so tedious that the device possesses little value either as an efficient means of handling syllogisms or in giving the mind a clear visual understanding of what is happening in syllogistic inference. In such respects it is markedly inferior to the Venn circles, which in some ways it anticipates. On the other hand, owing to its rectangular form, it is more efficient than the Venn circles when used for syllogisms with terms that have numerically definite quantifiers or indefinite quantifiers such as "more than half" or "less than half."

Consider, for example, these premises:

Some *M* is some *A*
Some *M* is some *B*

The gray panel is "some *A*"; the red is "some *B*." Each is pushed only part way over the holon (some *M*). The two slides are not forced to overlap; hence no conclusion can be drawn. Suppose, however, that for "some *M*" in each premise we substitute "most of *M*." In this case, each slide is made to cover "most," or more than half of the holon, and it is apparent that they must overlap to some extent. We therefore can conclude validly that "Some *A* is *B*." This is, of course, an example of one of De Morgan's syllogisms discussed in the second chapter.

To illustrate how the demonstrator may be used for De Morgan's syllogism with numerical quantifiers, let us consider what can be deduced from the following two premises:

8 of 10 pictures are abstractions.
4 of the same 10 pictures are by Picasso.

We let the holon stand for the middle term of "10 pictures." The gray slide (8 abstractions) is pushed in from the left until its right edge reaches 8 on the top scale. In other words, until it covers $8/10$ of the area of the holon. The red slide (4 pictures by Picasso) is pushed in from the right until the number 4 on its lower scale coincides with the right edge of the holon; in other words, until it covers $4/10$ of the holon. Through the red glass we see immediately that the edge of the gray slide is touching the 2 on the red slide's scale, indicating that the overlapping area is $2/10$ of the holon. This is what Stanhope calls, on the face of his device, the "extent of the consequence," namely, the minimum number of objects that belong to both the *ho* and the *los*. Our conclusion, then, is that *at least* two of the abstractions must be by Picasso. Of course there may be more (four is the upper limit because there are only four Picasso pictures), but the demonstrator neatly provides us with a visual demonstration of why two is the lower limit.

If the middle term is less than ten units—say, six units—then we simply regard as our holon only that portion of the aperture which extends from the left side to 6 on the upper scale. The gray slide is unaffected by this, but when we use the red slide we must remember to bring the desired number on its lower edge to the point indicated by 6 on the upper scale rather than to the right edge of the holon. It is clear that numerical syllogisms with terms quantified by numbers higher than ten could be handled in exactly the same manner on demonstrators with scales divided into a larger number of units.

In Stanhope's terminology, the demonstrator operates mechanically on all types of syllogisms according to the following simple rule: "Add *ho* to *los* and subtract *holos*." The machine shows clearly how the rule applies, regardless of whether the terms of the syllogism are quantified by numbers, more or less than half, or "all" and "some."

"Behold, then," the Earl writes in one of his notes, "the luminous perspicuity and most beautiful simplicity of this new system of logic!"

Stanhope's letters and unpublished papers do not give examples of how he used his device for his "logic of probability," but from the rule given at the bottom of the brass face (see Figure 74), it is easy to understand how the instrument must have been employed on such problems. This rule states, "The proportion between the area of the dark red [that is, the overlapping area of the two slides] and the area of the holon, is the probability which results from the gray and red."

Rev. Harley illustrates this in his article with the following elementary problem. We wish to determine the probability that a penny will fall heads both times if we toss it twice.

The holon represents 1 or "certainty." The probability of a head in a single throw is one-half. To show this, the gray slide is removed from the slot on the left, inserted through the slot at the top, then pushed down until its edge reaches 5 on the left-hand scale; that is, until it covers one-half the area of the holon. To represent the chance of a head on the second toss, the red slide is pushed to the left until it also covers one-half the area of the holon. The dark red, or overlapping area of the two slides, is obviously one-fourth of the holon. The chance that the penny will fall heads on both tosses is therefore one-fourth. The same procedure would be used, Harley points out, to give exactly the same answer, if we wanted to know the probability that the coin would fall tails twice, or heads and then tails, or tails and then heads.

As in dealing with numerical syllogisms, probability problems involving fractions that cannot be expressed in tenths could be suitably handled by giving the device whatever type of scale it required. Used in this manner, Stanhope's device can be viewed as an extremely crude first attempt at the kind of inductive machine mentioned briefly in Chapter 9.

If for your own amusement you wish to make a demonstrator, Rev. Harley suggests a simple way to go about it. Draw on a sheet of graph paper a square consisting of 100 smaller squares and

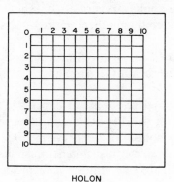

HOLON

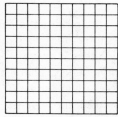 

GRAY SLIDE   RED SLIDE

Figures 75 (top), 76, and 77.

label the lattice lines above and on the left as shown in Figure 75. For the gray slide, use a similar square (Figure 76), and for the red slide, a square with a scale indicated on the bottom edge as shown in Figure 77. Harley suggests trimming the lower edge of this square as pictured, so that, when it overlaps the other square, the extent of overlapping can be clearly seen. If you wish, you can color this slide red, and of course all three squares may be mounted on cardboard to make them more durable. They obviously are capable of performing any operation that can be performed on the Stanhope device.

References

1. Stanhope had three daughters by his first wife. The youngest created a scandal by eloping with the family druggist. The Earl was never reconciled to the pair, but Prime Minister Pitt made the druggist controller-general of the customs. The eldest daughter, Lady Hester Lucy Stanhope (1776–1839), kept house for Pitt until his death in 1806. In 1814, with a generous pension from the government, she settled in an abandoned convent in Lebanon where until her death she ruled over her retinue of some thirty servants like an Oriental potentate. For a time she was a political power in the Syrian area. In later years, her interest in the occult intensified, and she claimed to be an inspired prophetess. For fascinating accounts of her beauty, sarcastic wit, arrogance, and legendary exploits, see Alphonse de Lamartine's *Voyages en Orient,* Alexander Kinglake's *Eothen,* and the six volumes of Lady Hester's memoirs prepared after her death by her physician, Dr. Charles Lewis Meryon.

   The fourth Earl Stanhope, Philip Henry (one of Charles's three sons by his second wife), is best known for his espousal of the famous German imposter, Kaspar Hauser. Philip paid for Hauser's education and even wrote a book in German about him.

2. Lord Stanhope either made or had made for him several models of both his logic and arithmetical machines. Photographs of one model of each machine are reproduced opposite page 127 of *Early Science in Oxford,* by Robert W. T. Gunther, Vol. 1, Part 1, 1922. These two models are owned by the Oxford Museum of the History of Science, Old Ashmolean Building, Oxford. A second model of the logic machine is owned by the present Earl Stanhope.

3. A quotation from one of Stanhope's letters gives an amusing insight into the value he placed on recognizing that class propositions could be expressed as identities:

   "When I talk of identity, I do *not* say, as you make me say, *que 'L'âme est l'âme,' car cela ne dit rien,* but I say thus: Example. Suppose I had heard that there was such a thing as a *comet.* I now perceive in the heavens at night *a star with a luminous tail;* that is all I know, and it is by means of that mental description that I distinguish that star from all other stars. I afterwards find my star, so distinguished, described and defined, amongst the stars of some new constellation, and I predicate that that star *has moved fast,* which is a quality of my comet, but which quality of my comet was before to me unknown; that is to say, I aver that 'the star with a luminous tail' and a star which 'moves fast,' that is, which belongs to the *class of stars that move fast,* are IDENTIC. Have I not made an advance in knowledge by my having so perceived, though in point of fact, it is the *same* comet, the *identical* comet, originally described by me incompletely, before I perceived, or could predicate, such identity? *Voilà tout.* Would it not sound to your ears very droll if a person were to say that *that star moving fast* means that it is identic with some star which does *not move fast?* Now if that would be evidently wrong, and if I have by my method *only two opposite classes, viz.,* stars *moving fast* and stars *not moving fast,* if the proposition in question does not mean that the given star is *identic* with a star in the second class, it must mean that it is identic with a star in the first class; for there are *two* classes only. This is my induction in other words."

5: Jevons's Logic Machine

Ramon Lull was the first to use a mechanical device as an aid to reasoning. Lord Stanhope was the first to use a mechanical device for the solution of problems in formal logic. The next great step in the history of logic machines took place in 1869 when William Stanley Jevons, British economist and logician, produced the first working model of his famous logic machine. It was the first such machine with sufficient power to solve a complicated problem faster than the problem could be solved without the machine's aid.

Jevons was born in Liverpool in 1835, the son of an iron merchant. He interrupted his education at University College, London, to spend five years working for the British mint in Sidney, Australia. In 1859 he returned to University College and, after obtaining a master of arts degree, accepted the post of tutor at Owens College, now the University of Manchester. He soon found himself carrying the double title of "professor of logic and mental and moral philosophy" and "professor of political economy." In 1876 he became professor of political economy at his alma mater, the University College, London, where he remained until he resigned the chair in 1880 because of failing health. Two years later, at the age of only forty-seven, he was drowned while swimming alone off the beach at Bulverhythe, near Hastings.

As an economist, Jevons is regarded as one of the pioneers in the rigorous application of statistical techniques to the study of economic issues. His *Theory of Political Economy,* 1871, is the most important of his many books and papers on economic and political topics. Unfortunately, his valuable contributions to economic theory (especially his trenchant analysis of marginal utility) are less well remembered today than his speculations on the relation of sunspots to business cycles. In the light of present-day knowledge and statistical sophistication, such a theory can only be regarded as eccentric, but we must remember that in Jevons's time it was far from a crank notion. The view that sunspots might influence weather and crops, which in turn would affect the business cycle, then had a plausibility that deserved careful exploration.[1]

In somewhat similar fashion, Jevons's fame as the inventor of a logic machine has tended to obscure the important role he played in the history of both deductive and inductive logic. He was one of the pioneers of modern symbolic logic, and his *Principles of Science,* first issued in 1874, deserves far more recognition than it has today as an important treatise on the philosophy and methods of science. At a time when most British logicians ignored or damned with faint praise the remarkable achievements of George Boole, Jevons was quick to see the importance of Boole's work as well as many of its defects. He regarded Boole's algebraic logic as the greatest advance in the history of the subject since Aristotle. He deplored the fact that Boole's two revolutionary books, published as early as 1847 and 1854, had virtually no effect on the speculations of leading logicians of the time.

On the other hand, Jevons believed (and modern logicians agree with him) that Boole had been led astray by efforts to make his logical notation resemble algebraic notation. "I am quite convinced," Jevons stated in a letter, "that Boole's forms . . . have no real analogy to the similar mathematical expressions."[2] He also saw clearly the weakness in Boole's preference for the exclusive rather than the inclusive interpretation of "or."

It was to overcome what he regarded as unnecessary obscurity and awkwardness in Boole's notation that Jevons devised a method of his own that he called the "method of indirect inference." "I have been able to arrive at exactly the same results as Dr. Boole," he wrote, "without the use of any mathematics; and though the very simple process which I am about to describe can hardly be said to be strictly Dr. Boole's logic, it is yet very similar to it and can prove everything that Dr. Boole proved."[3] Jevons's system, as we shall see, is also very similar to Venn's diagrammatic method as well as a primitive form of the familiar matrix or truth-table technique. Since it underlies Jevons's logic machine, it will be necessary to review it in some detail.

Putting it jocularly, but with a certain amount of justification, one might say that the method is a linking of Lull's *Ars magna* with one of Sherlock Holmes's favorite canons of deduction; namely, that if you eliminate all possible explanations of a crime but one, that one explanation is certain to be correct. As the technique of *reductio ad absurdum,* this procedure is an ancient one, but the realization that it could be applied to the Boolean logic came to Jevons in an almost Lullian-like illumination. "As I awoke in the morning," he recorded in his journal in 1866, "the sun was shining brightly into my room. There was a consciousness on my mind that I was the discoverer of the true logic of the future. For a few minutes I felt a delight such as one can seldom hope to feel." [4]

The easiest way to explain Jevons's logic is to give a few examples of how it operates. Let us consider first the two syllogistic premises, All *A* is *B,* and No *B* is *C.* Our first step is to make a Lullian table that exhausts all possible combinations of *ABC* and their negations. Since Jevons always symbolized a negation by using a lower-case letter (a convention which he borrowed from De Morgan) we shall adopt this practice here. The table appears as follows:

ABC
ABc
AbC
Abc
aBC
aBc
abC
abc

These eight classes correspond of course to the eight compartments of Venn's three-circle diagram (including the area representing *abc,* which lies outside the circles). Jevons at first called such an exhaustive list an "abecedarium," but students found this difficult to pronounce so he soon discarded it for "logical alphabet." [5] His procedure for analyzing the two premises corresponds precisely with Venn's procedure in shading compartments on the intersecting circles.[6] The first premise, All *A* is *B*, tells us that the classes *Abc* and *AbC* are empty; therefore we draw a line through them. Similarly, the second premise, No *B* is *C*, will eliminate classes *ABC* and *aBC*. The logical alphabet will now look like this:

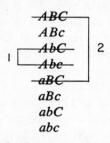

The final step is to inspect the remaining classes, all consistent with the premises, to see what we can determine about the relation of *A* to *C*. We note at once that "No *A* is *C*" (that is, there are no remaining combinations containing both *A* and *C*); hence this is a valid inference from the premises. On the assumption that none of the three classes are empty, we may also conclude that "Some *A* is not *C*," since the only class containing an *A* is one that contains a *c*. This is what classic logic calls a "weak" conclusion because it can be derived by immediate inference from the universal conclusion "No *A* is *C*." We may also draw various other non-traditional inferences such as "Some not-*A* is *C*." Like Venn and Lewis Carroll, Jevons was proud of the fact that his system was not limited to the traditional syllogistic conclusions, providing all possible inferences from the original premises.

In handling particular ("some") statements, the logical alphabet does not operate as smoothly as the Venn circles. The premise "Some *A* is *B*" does not eliminate any classes, but simply states that, of the two combinations *ABc* and *ABC*, at least one and possibly both have members. Perhaps the best procedure is to draw circles around these combinations (corresponding to the placing of *X*'s in the cells of Venn circles), remembering that, when two classes are circled, they cannot both be empty. Jevons suggested some other procedures for handling these troublesome "somes," all rather clumsy and of no special interest.

In working with binary truth-value relations, Jevons's system operates more efficiently than with class logic. In explaining its application to the propositional calculus we shall take the same liberties we took in explaining how the Venn diagrams could be similarly used. Like Venn and most of the other logicians of his time, Jevons confined his attention almost exclusively to class logic. He combined statements of class inclusion (though he preferred, like Stanhope, to think of such statements in terms of identity of part or all of one class with part or all of another) with conjunctive or disjunctive assertions (e.g., All A and B is either C or D) but almost never worked with truth-value relations alone.

The trend toward a truth-value calculus was making a faint beginning in Jevons's time, but unfortunately he failed completely to see its significance.[7] Perhaps, like Boole, he was too intent on keeping his notation in the form of equations. For example, Jevons's expression for the statement "All A is B" is the equation $A = AB$, meaning that all of class A is identical with the class of things that are both A and B. This equational form then permitted him to substitute for any term or statement any other term or statement that was equivalent. Jevons called this "the substitution of similars." (Statements were "similar" for him if they removed the same combinations from his logical alphabet. Modern logicians would call them equivalent or tautological.) The following passage from his *Studies in Deductive Logic*, p. xv, in which he refers to the new calculus of Hugh MacColl,[8] reveals how decisively Jevons turned his back on the trend toward truth-value analysis:

> Mr. MacColl rejects equations in favor of *implications;* thus my $A = AB$ becomes with him $A:B$, or A implies B. Even his letter-terms differ in meaning from mine, since his letters denote propositions, not things. Thus $A:B$ asserts that the statement A implies the statement B, or that whenever A is true, B is also true. It is difficult to believe that there is any advantage in these innovations; certainly, in preferring implications to equations, Mr. MacColl ignores the necessity of the equation for the application of the Principle of Substitution. His proposals seem to me to tend towards throwing Formal Logic back into its ante-Boolian confusion.

Because of his preference for what he called "equational logic," we shall look in vain through Jevons's works for problems of a truth-value nature. Ironically, these are precisely the problems that are the easiest to solve by his method. The following simple examples should make clear how such problems are handled. We are given these premises:

> If and only if A is true, then B is true.
> Either B or C, but not both, are true.
> A is false.

We wish to know what we may infer about B and C.

As before, the first step is to write down the logical alphabet for three terms. The first premise tells us that we must eliminate all combinations containing Ab and aB. The second premise eliminates all combinations containing BC and bc.[9] The third premise excludes all combinations containing A. The alphabet will now look like this:

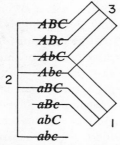

Inspection of the one remaining line of the alphabet shows clearly that B must be false and C true.

The method is essentially the same as the method described in Chapter 2 by which Venn circles may be used for truth-value logic. Both methods correspond closely to a truth-table analysis. The logical alphabet is simply another way of symbolizing all the possible combinations of truth values. Each premise forces us to eliminate certain lines of this "truth table." What remain are of course the lines that are consistent with the premises. If the premises contain a contradiction, then all the lines will be eliminated just as all the compartments will become shaded if contradictory truth-value premises are diagramed on Venn circles.[10] Jevons likes to call his system a "combinatorial logic," and although he did not apply it to propositional functions, he clearly grasped the principles of matrix analysis that had eluded Boole even though it was implied in his formula for expanding a function. Dr. Wolfe Mays, senior lecturer in philosophy at the University of Manchester (and, as we shall learn later, a coinventor of England's first electric logic machine), is of the opinion that Jevons was the first to make use of matrix analysis.[11]

To increase the efficiency of his combinatorial method, Jevons devised a number of laborsaving devices, culminating in the construction of his logic machine. For example, he suggested having a rubber stamp made of the logical alphabet for three terms, another stamp for four. This eliminates the annoyance of having to jot down all the combinations each time you tackle a new problem. For a problem of five terms, you have only to make two impressions with the *ABCD* stamp, heading one of them *E* and the other *e*. (Venn also suggested having rubber stamps made for his circular figures. See his *Symbolic Logic*, revised 1894 edition, p. 135.)

As early as 1863 Jevons was using a "logical slate." This was a slate on which a logical alphabet was permanently engraved so that problems could be solved by chalking out the inconsistent lines. Still another device, suggested to Jevons by a correspondent, is to pencil the alphabet along the extreme edge of a sheet of paper, then cut the sheet between each pair of adjacent combinations. When a combination is to be eliminated, it is simply folded back out of sight.

Jevons's "logical abacus" (most fully described in his book *The Substitution of Similars*, 1869) was a laborsaving device that required only the addition of keys, levers, and pulleys to become a logic machine. The abacus consisted of small rectangular wooden boards, all the same size, and each bearing a different combination of true and false terms. The boards were lined up on a rack. An arrangement of pegs on the side of each board was such that one could insert a ruler under the pegs and quickly pick out whatever group of boards one wished to remove from the rack. The device was really a primitive form of an IBM punch-card machine, and suggests how easily such a sorting mechanism could be adapted to solving logic problems by the Jevons method.

Jevons's "logical piano," as he sometimes called the machine, was built for him by a "young clockmaker in Salford" in 1869.[12] The following year he demonstrated the machine at a meeting of the Royal Society of London, explaining its construction and working in a paper titled "On the Mechanical Performance of Logical Inference." The paper was printed in full, together with plates showing details of the machine's construction, in the society's *Philosophical Transactions,* Vol. 160, 1870, p. 497. This paper was later reprinted in Jevons's posthumously published *Pure Logic and Other Minor Works,* 1890. (Summaries of the paper appeared in the society's *Proceedings,* Vol. 18, Jan. 20, 1870, p. 166, and in *Nature,* Vol. 1, Jan. 27, 1870, p. 343.)

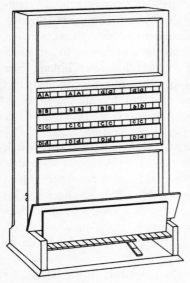

In appearance Jevons's machine resembles a miniature upright piano about 3 feet high (Figure 78). On the face of the piano are openings through which one can see letters representing the 16 possible combinations of four terms and their negatives. (Each combination forms a vertical row of four terms.) The keyboard consists of 21 keys arranged as shown in Figure 79.

Figure 78. Jevons's logic machine. (From frontispiece of *Principles of Science,* 1874, by William S. Jevons.)

The four terms, in positive and negative forms, are represented by eight "letter keys" on the left, and eight letter keys in mirror-image order on the right. The remaining five keys are called "operation keys." The "copula" in the center is pressed to indicate the sign of equality connecting left and right sides of an equation. The "full stop" on the extreme right is pressed after a complete equation has been fed to the machine. When the "finis" key on the ex-

FINIS	·|·	d	D	c	C	b	B	a	A	COPULA	A	a	B	b	C	c	D	d	·|·	FULL STOP

Figure 79.

treme left is pressed, it restores the machine to its original condition. The next-to-end keys on both sides represent the inclusive "or" which Jevons symbolized by ·|·. They are used whenever the "or" relation occurs within either the left or right sides of an equation.

To operate the machine it is only necessary to press the keys in the order indicated by the terms of an equation. For example, let us consider the equation $A = AB$, which as we have seen was Jevons's notation for "All A is B." To feed this to the machine we press the following keys in order: A (on the left), copula, A (on the right), B (on the right), full stop. This action automatically eliminates from the face of the machine all combinations of terms inconsistent with the proposition just fed to the machine. Additional equations are handled in exactly the same manner. After all premises have been fed to the device, its face is then inspected to determine what conclusions can be drawn. This is by no means a complete description of the technique for operating the machine, but it should suffice to indicate in a general way how the machine is handled. The interested reader can learn further details by consulting the references cited above.

Jevons did not think that his machine had any practical use, owing to the fact that complex logical questions seldom arise in everyday life. But he did feel that it was valuable as a classroom device for demonstrating the nature of logical analysis, and also that it furnished a convincing proof of the superiority of Boolean logic over that of Aristotle. The following lengthy quotation (*Principles of Science*, pp. 113 ff.) is striking because it reveals how clearly Jevons grasped the revolutionary character of Boole's work as well as many of its defects:

The time must come when the inevitable results of the admirable investigations of the late Dr. Boole must be recognized at their true value, and the plain and palpable form in which the machine presents those results will, I hope, hasten the time. Undoubtedly Boole's life marks an era in the science of human reason. It may seem strange that it had remained for him first to set forth in its full extent the problem of logic, but I am not aware that anyone before him had treated logic as a symbolic method for evolving from any premises the description of any class whatsoever as defined by those premises. In spite of several serious errors into which he fell, it will probably be allowed that Boole discovered the true and general form of logic, and put the science substantially into the form which it must hold for evermore. He thus effected a reform with which there is hardly anything comparable in the history of logic between his time and the remote age of Aristotle.

Nevertheless, Boole's quasi-mathematical system could hardly be regarded as a final and unexceptionable solution of the problem. Not only did it require the manipulation of mathematical symbols in a very intricate and perplexing manner, but the results when obtained were devoid of demonstrative force, because they turned upon the employment of unintelligible symbols, acquiring meaning only by analogy. I have also pointed out that he imported into his system a condition concerning the exclusive nature of alternatives, which is not necessarily true of logical terms. I shall have to show in the next chapter that logic is really the basis of the whole science of mathematical reasoning, so that Boole inverted the true order of proof when he proposed to infer logical truths by algebraic processes. It is wonderful evidence of his mental power that by methods fundamentally false he should have succeeded in reaching true conclusions and widening the sphere of reason.

The mechanical performance of logical inference affords a demonstration both of the truth of Boole's results and of the mistaken nature of his mode of deducing them. Conclusions which he could obtain only by pages of intricate calculation, are exhibited by the machine after one or two minutes of manipulation. And not only are those conclusions easily reached, but they are demonstratively true, because every step of the process involves nothing more obscure than the three fundamental Laws of Thought.

It is not surprising that Jevons's logic machine, being the first of its kind, would have defects that could be remedied by later machines operating on essentially the same principles. By insisting that statements be fed to the machine in a clumsy equational form, it is made unnecessarily complicated. There is no efficient procedure for feeding "some" propositions to the machine. The mechanism does not permit of easy extension to a larger number of terms. (Jevons once contemplated building a machine for ten terms but abandoned the project when it became clear that the device would occupy the entire wall space of one side of his study.)

A more serious objection to the machine, and one that may not permit of remedy within the framework of Jevons's combinatorial logic, was voiced by the British philosopher Francis H. Bradley in a section on the machine in his *The Principles of Logic*, 1883. As a conclusion, the machine merely exhibits all the consistent lines of the logical alphabet (i.e., all the valid lines of a truth table for the combined premises). It does not perform the additional step of analyzing these lines so that one can see the desired conclusion. The process of analyzing the consistent combinations to determine which terms are true and which are false, or even to find the conclusion of a syllogism, is often as laborious as solving the problem itself. In many cases the valid combinations will not provide true and false values for individual terms but will give a series of consistent combinations that can be condensed into a simpler, more "powerful" logical statement. For example, the machine may reveal the following valid combinations: *AB*, *Ab*, *aB*. It does not have the power to reduce this answer to the simpler statement, "Either *A* or *B*, or both, are true" (*A* v *B*). In simple cases such as this, one can easily see the relation that is involved, but in more complicated cases, the task of reducing the answer to compact form is not an easy one. In *Principles of Science* Jevons discusses this task in terms of what he calls the "inverse problem," identifying it (not very successfully) with the process of induction. He does not relate the problem to his machine, though clearly it would be of great value to have a mechanical method of performing these desired reductions.

Jevons himself suggested a crude pencil and paper technique of reducing statements (*Principles of Science*, p. 139) comparing it with the "sieve of Eratosthenes" by which one can search for prime numbers. Later logicians have devised better methods, and although no mechanical device has been built for performing these operations, we shall see in Chapter 8 that electric "minimizing machines" have been constructed.

References

1. In a study of British trade from 1721 to 1878 Jevons found 16 crises in 157 years, giving an average cycle of 10.466 which corresponded closely to estimates in his time of the sunspot cycle. A more complicated version of the theory was set forth by Jevons's son in 1909 to accommodate new data that did not conform to his father's theory. After that, works on the solar causes of boom and bust seem to appear in cycles of 4½ years.

   Owing to vagueness in deciding what constitutes a crisis and exactly when it begins and ends, it is as easy to squeeze economic data into a desired pattern as it is to squeeze historical facts into the construction of the Great Pyramid of Egypt. Henry L. Moore, a Columbia University economist, in a book published in 1923, found an eight-year business cycle which he correlated with the transits of Venus across the sun. Harvard economist Felix I. Shaffner, in the November, 1934, issue of the *Quarterly Journal of Economics,* correlated depressions with sunspots. Two major busts that did not fit his pattern were blamed on volcanic eruptions that screened off solar radiation by filling the atmosphere with dust. Shaffner predicted the next great depression in 1944.

   More recently, *Sunspots in Action,* by Harlan T. Stetson of the Massachusetts Institute of Technology, linked economic depression to mental depression, in turn conditioned by a ten-year sunspot cycle. Stetson warned against the next big crash in 1951.

2. *The Letters and Journal of W. Stanley Jevons,* 1886, p. 350. The book is edited by Jevons's wife who, it is interesting to note, was the daughter of the founder and first owner of the *Manchester Guardian.*

3. *Elementary Lessons in Logic*, 1870, Lesson 23. No English logic text has enjoyed a wider popularity than this. It has had 35 reprintings and is still in print.

4. Quoted by W. Mays and D. P. Henry in their excellent exposition of Jevons's logical views, "Jevons and Logic," *Mind*, Vol. 62, October, 1953, p. 484.

5. Jevons was much intrigued by the formal properties of his logical alphabet. In *Principles of Science* he devotes considerable space to showing its similarities to Pascal's triangle of numbers, and emphasizing that its underlying duality is simply another version of the ancient practice of classifying things by a principle of dichotomy. "Some interest attaches to the history of the Tree of Porphyry and Ramus," he writes, "because it is the prototype of the Logical Alphabet which lies at the basis of logical method" (p. 703).

6. Jevons's method was worked out before Venn's diagrammatic procedure; so there is more justification for regarding the Venn circles as a diagrammatic form of Jevons's alphabet than the alphabet as a notational method of handling Venn's system. Both men, however, looked upon their respective systems as stemming from the work of Boole.

7. This is not meant to imply that the logic of propositions had its origin in this trend. There are hints of such a logic as far back as Aristotle. In the Stoic-Megaric school it reached a high stage of development, including explicit recognition of different kinds of implication, of disjunction in both exclusive and inclusive forms, as well as other truth-value functions and a number of elementary equivalence formulas. The Stoic-Megaric school was as disinterested in Aristotle's class logic as any modern logician. Sextus Empiricus quotes a third century B.C. remark by the head of the Alexandrian Library, that "even the crows on the rooftops are cawing over which conditional is true." See chap. 15 of *Ancient Formal Logic*, by I. M. Bocheński, Amsterdam, 1951.

8. MacColl made many valuable contributions toward an efficient notation for the propositional calculus in articles published only in British newspapers and magazines. Alonzo Church credits him with having developed the first true propositional calculus, and J. Barkley Rosser has recently called attention to MacColl's astonishing analysis, as early as 1896, of a three-value logic using the values "necessary," "impossible," and "possible but not necessary."

9. In one of his letters (*The Letters and Journal of W. Stanley Jevons*, p. 350) Jevons contrasts his notation for the exclusive "or" with Boole's notation to show the greater simplicity of his method over Boole's. Jevons used the symbol $\cdot|\cdot$ for inclusive disjunction. He was therefore able to express any binary relation by the simple expedient of using this symbol to join together the required combinations of true and false terms. Thus his notation for the exclusive "or" was $Ab \cdot|\cdot aB$. Boole's way of symbolizing the same relation was $x(1-y) + y(1-x)$. In *Studies in Deductive Logic* Jevons gives a complete matrix analysis of the 256 possible relations involving three terms, expressing each relation both in equational form and in terms of the valid lines of its truth table.

10. This holds only for the propositional calculus. In class logic a contradiction is revealed in two ways: (1) when all the combinations specified by a "some" proposition are eliminated by a universal proposition, and (2) when a class known to have members is declared empty by the elimination of all combinations containing the capital letter for that class.

11. The answer to the question of who was the first to use a matrix method depends of course on how broadly or narrowly the term "matrix method" is defined. As Venn points out (*Symbolic Logic,* revised 1894 edition, p. 415), C. A. Semler, in an 1811 German work, suggested the procedure of listing all possible combinations of terms, then striking out those that are contradicted by the premises, a clear anticipation of Jevons's method. If by "matrix method" we mean nothing more than recognition of the alternate possible combinations of truth values for a given binary function, then this recognition goes all the way back to the ancient Stoic-Megaric school. A truth table for material implication, for example, is given by Sextus Empiricus to define the meaning of a conditional statement as it was understood by Philo of Megara.

The fact remains, however, that Jevons was probably the first to make extensive use of what is substantially a truth-table method for solving problems, even though its first explicit application to truth-value statements came later. In Jevons's unpublished notes, Dr. W. Mays has pointed out, he even used the now familiar notational device of marking lines of his alphabet with 1 or 0 to indicate their truth or falsity.

12. In 1914 Jevons's original machine was given by his son to the Science Museum, South Kensington, London, but in 1934 it was transferred to the Oxford Museum of the History of Science, Old Ashmolean Building, Oxford, where it is now on display.

6: Marquand's Machine and Others

The Reverend John Venn did not have a high opinion of Jevons as a logician. "Excellent as much of Jevons' work is," Venn wrote (*Symbolic Logic*, revised 1894 edition, p. 165), "—especially as regards the principles of physical and economical science,—I cannot but hold that in the domain of logic his inconsistencies and contradictions are remarkable." There was a strong element of rivalry between the two men; hence it is not surprising to find Venn dismissing Jevons's logic machine as essentially trivial.

I have no high estimate myself [he writes, *op.cit.*, p. 133], of the interest or importance of what are sometimes called logical machines, and this on two grounds. In the first place, it is very seldom that intricate logical calculations are practically forced upon us; it is rather we who look about for complicated examples in order to illustrate our rules and methods. In this respect logical calculations stand in marked contrast with those of mathematics, where economical devices of any kind may subserve a really valuable purpose by enabling us to avoid otherwise inevitable labour. Moreover, in the second place, it does not seem to me that any contrivances at present known or likely to be discovered really deserve the name of logical machines. It is but a very small part of the entire process, which goes to form a piece of reasoning, which they are capable of performing. For, if we begin from the beginning, that process would involve four tolerably distinct steps. There is, first, the statement of our data in accurate logical language. This step deserves to be reckoned, since the variations of popular language are so multitudinous, and the terms often so ambiguous, that the data may need careful consideration before they can be reduced to form. Then, secondly, we have to throw these statements into a form fit for the engine to work with—in this case to reduce each proposition to its elementary denials. It would task the energies of any machine to deal at once with the premises employed even in such simple examples as we have offered, if they were presented to it in their original form. Thirdly, there is the combination or further treatment of our premises after such reduction. Finally, the results have to be interpreted or read off. This last generally gives rise to much opening for skill and sagacity; for . . . in most cases there are many ways of reading off the answer. It then becomes a question of tact and judgment which of these is the simplest and best. . . . I hardly see how any machine can hope to assist us except in the third of these steps; so that it seems very doubtful whether any thing of this sort really deserves the name of a logical engine.

Venn goes on to say that "So little trouble is required to sketch out a fresh diagram for ourselves on each occasion, that it is really not worth while to get a machine to do any part of the work for us. Still as some persons have felt much interest in such attempts, it seemed worth while seeing how the thing could be effected here." He then suggests several mechanical procedures of his own. First, the use of a rubber stamp to form the intersecting circles. Second, draw the desired diagrams on thin board, then cut out the compartments so they fit together like a jigsaw puzzle. Instead of shading compartments, you now can remove the cell in question. Third, he gives a picture (reproduced in Figure 80) of what he calls a "logical-diagram machine."

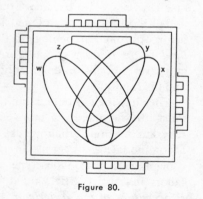

Figure 80.

This machine is merely a three-dimensional form of the jigsaw device. The individual pieces are parts of intersecting elliptical cylinders held in place at the top of a box by sixteen pegs on the sides of the box. To eliminate a cell, you pull out the proper peg, allowing the wooden piece to drop to the bottom of the box. The box is turned upside-down to bring all the blocks back into position for a fresh problem. The picture shows a cross section of the box looking down from above. You will note that the outside compartment is here represented by a closed cell held in place by the top left-hand peg. Venn was of the opinion that this device "would succeed in doing all that can be rationally expected of any logic machine."

As Venn himself recognized, his logic box was simply a mechanical way of handling a Venn diagram. It is surprising that Venn did not think of placing counters on his diagrams, after the manner of Lewis Carroll's method, since this is much simpler than the contrivances he proposed and has the additional advantage that counters of two different colors may be used—one to show that a cell has no members, the other to indicate cells involved in particular ("some") assertions. Although it is true that Venn's devices can perform any of the operations possible on Jevons's logic machine, Venn would not permit himself to appreciate the fact that Jevons's machine was a pioneer effort to work out a mechanical laborsaving method in which desired operations could be effected merely by pressing keys.

The first real advance over Jevons's machine was made by Allan Marquand (1853–1924). The son of Henry G. Marquand, a prominent American philanthropist and art collector, Allan Marquand began his teaching career as a fellow in logic and ethics at Johns Hopkins University. He became a tutor of logic at Princeton University in 1881, but soon abandoned logic to become (in 1883) a professor of art and archeology at Princeton. His books include a *Textbook of the History of Sculpture*, 1896; *Greek Architecture*, 1909; and several books on della Robbia, the famous Florentine sculptor, and his family.

The first logical device built by Marquand is of no special interest. It was merely a more elaborate version of Venn's logical-diagram machine, making use of 256 separate wooden parts to accommodate eight terms. In 1881 he turned his attention toward a machine of the Jevons type, describing the final outcome of his labors in a brief article titled "A New Logical Machine," in the *Proceedings of the American Academy of Arts and Sciences*, Vol. 21, 1885, p. 303. The following account of his machine is taken from this paper.

A crude first model was built by Marquand some time in 1881; then during the winter of 1881–1882 an improved and final model was constructed for Marquand by his friend Prof. Charles G. Rockwood, Jr., of Princeton's department of mathematics. "The machine was made from the wood of a red-cedar post," Marquand tells us, "which once formed part of the enclosure of Princeton's oldest homestead."

Photographs of front and back views of this machine, as it appears today, are reproduced in Figures 81 and 82. In external appearance it resembles a smaller version of Jevons's "logical piano," standing only a trifle more than a foot high, about eight inches wide, and six inches from front to back. The inner mechanism (Figure 82) consists of an ingenious arrangement of rods and

Figure 81. Marquand's logic machine, front view.

Figure 82. Marquand's logic machine, back view, opened to show interior.

levers connected by catgut strings, together with small pins and spiral springs.

Like Jevons's machine it is designed for four terms. The sixteen possible combinations of true and false terms are represented by sixteen rotating pointers on the face of the machine. These pointers are labeled in accordance with Marquand's logic diagram which he had described in a paper published earlier in 1881 (see Figure 33). The method of labeling is easily understood. The pointer in the upper left corner (see Figure 81) stands for *ABCD*. Next to it on the right *AbCD*, then *aBcD*, and so on until *abcd* is reached at the lower right corner. Each pointer can be raised to a horizontal position, pointing leftward, to indicate that the combination is "true" (consistent with the premises), or dropped to a vertical position, pointing downward, to indicate a "false" combination (one excluded by the premises).

The keyboard consists of ten keys only, labeled as shown in Figure 83.

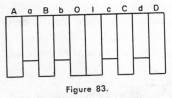

Figure 83.

The four terms (capital letters) and their negatives (lower case letters) are represented by eight keys, the keys for the negatives being shorter than the others. The remaining two keys, marked 1 (the "restoration key") and 0 (the "destruction key"), are called "operation keys." Their use will become clear in a moment.

Before a problem is fed to the machine, all pointers must first be raised to horizontal position. This is done by pressing the two operation keys simultaneously, then releasing first the 1 key, then the 0 key.

Each premise is now fed to the machine in negative form. For example, suppose we wish to impress upon the machine the premise $A \supset B$. This can be restated in negative form by saying that a true A cannot combine with a false B. In other words, all combinations containing Ab must be eliminated from the face of the machine. This is simply done as follows. We press simultaneously the keys for A and b; then while still holding them down with one hand, the other hand presses the 0, or destruction, key. Immediately all pointers representing combinations containing Ab drop to a vertical position. The face of the machine then appears as shown in Figure 84.

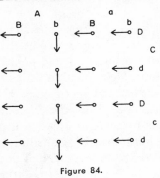

Figure 84.

Each succeeding premise is handled in exactly the same manner. After all premises have been fed to the machine the pointers indicate what combinations, if any, are consistent with the premises, and desired conclusions can be obtained by inspection of the machine's face. In principle, therefore, the machine operates as does Jevons device by identifying the valid lines of Jevons's "logical alphabet" or wha in modern terms would be called the "true" lines of a truth table for the combined premises.

The machine is a decided improvement over Jevons's. By abandoning the clumsy equational form which Jevons used, Marquand was able to cut down the number of keys to less than half of the 21 keys required on Jevons's model. In addition, the number of steps for feeding each premise to the machine is enormously reduced. A third advantage is that the simplified interior mechanism makes it possible to construct similar machines for more than four terms without enlarging the device to giant, unwieldy proportions. Charles Peirce, in an article on "Logical Machines" (*American Journal of Psychology*, Vol. 1, November, 1887, p. 165), summarizes these advantages in the following interesting and characteristic manner:

> Mr. Marquand's machine is a vastly more clear-headed contrivance than that of Jevons. The nature of the problem has been grasped in a more masterly manner, and the directest possible means are chosen for the solution of it. In the machines actually constructed only four letters have been used, though there would have been no inconvenience in embracing six. Instead of using the cumbrous equations of Jevons, Mr. Marquand uses Professor Mitchell's method throughout.[1] There are virtually no keys except the eight for the letters and their negatives, for two keys used in the process of erasing, etc., should not count. Any number of keys may be put down together, in which case the corresponding letters are added, or they may be put down successively, in which case the corresponding combinations are multiplied. There is a sort of diagram face, showing the combinations or logical products as in Jevons's machine, but with the very important difference that the two dimensions of the plane are taken advantage of to arrange the combinations in such a way that the substance of the result is instantly seen. To work a simple syllogism, two pressures of the keys only are necessary, two keys being pressed each time. A cord has also to be pulled each time so as to actualize the statement which the pressure of the keys only formulates. This is good logic: philosophers are too apt to forget this cord to be pulled, this element of brute force in existence, and thus to regard the *solvet ambulando* as illogical. To work the syllogism with Mr. Jevons's machine requires ten successive movements, owing to the relatively clumsy manner in which the problem has been conceived.

Like Jevons's machine, Marquand's does not readily handle syllogisms involving "some" statements, but syllogisms with universal premises are taken care of easily. The premises of *Barbara*, for example—All *A* is *B*, All *B* is *C*—are fed to the machine in the negative form of:

$$Ab = 0$$
$$Bc = 0$$

The horizontal pointers then indicate the following four valid combinations:

ABC
aBC
abC
abc

If we examine the above combinations for the relation between A and C we find that only the combination of Ac does not appear. This tells us that "All A is C," the traditional conclusion of *Barbara*.

To illustrate how the machine handles the propositional calculus, Marquand cites two novel problems. Although he does not speak of them as examples of propositional logic, they are problems that today would be interpreted in truth-value rather than in class terms. They show that Marquand grasped much more clearly than did Jevons the ease with which propositional logic could be handled on a device of this type.

The first problem is stated by Marquand as follows:

Let us suppose that there are four girls at school, Anna, Bertha, Cora, and Dora, and that someone had observed that:
(1) Whenever either Anna or Bertha (or both) remained at home, Cora was at home; and
(2) When Bertha was out, Anna was out; and
(3) Whenever Cora was at home, Anna was at home.
What information is here conveyed concerning Dora?

To solve this problem we let A, B, C, D stand for the four girls, each letter corresponding to the initial of a girl's name. A capital letter indicates "at home" and a lower-case letter indicates the negative value of "not at home." (Since a girl must be either home or out, we have here two mutually exclusive values which permit us to put the problem into truth-value terms.)

The three premises, expressed by the symbols we have used in previous chapters, are:

1. $(A \lor B) \supset C$
2. $\sim B \supset \sim A$
3. $C \supset A$

Converting these to the required negative form and using Marquand's symbolism, we have:

1. $Ac = 0$
   $Bc = 0$
2. $bA = 0$
3. $Ca = 0$

When these four statements are fed to the machine, the face will appear as in Figure 85. An examination of the pointers, to determine what can be inferred about Dora, reveals that:

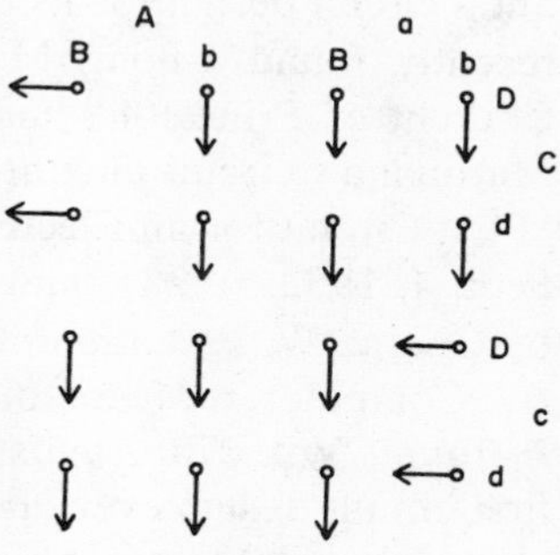

D may combine with either *ABC* or *abc*.
d also may combine with either *ABC* or *abc*.

In other words, when Dora is at home the other three girls are either all at home or all out. And the same holds true when Dora is out.

Marquand's second problem is: if $A \equiv B$ and $B \equiv C$, what can be said of *D*? The first premise eliminates *Ab* and *aB* from the face of the machine; the second eliminates *Bc* and *bC*. Oddly enough, the face will then appear exactly as it did after impressing upon the machine the premises of the preceding problem (Figure 85). As Marquand puts it, the two problems seem to be quite different but actually describe the "same state of the logical universe." They are merely two ways of expressing an identical structure of relations involving four terms.

While preparing this chapter in 1956 I wrote to Princeton University in an effort to learn the present whereabouts of Marquand's historic machine, the first device of its kind to be constructed in the United States. No one in either the philosophy or psychology departments had the slightest notion of where it might be. An extensive search finally uncovered it in the stacks of the university library. It had been presented to the library several years earlier by Marquand's descendants, together with sixteen cartons of as yet un-

Figure 85.

classified scrapbooks, documents, and correspondence belonging to Marquand.

James Mark Baldwin, in an article on "Logical Machines" (in his *Dictionary of Philosophy and Psychology*, 1902) writes:

> In 1882 Marquand constructed from an ordinary hotel annunciator another machine in which all the combinations are visible at the outset, and the inconsistent combinations are concealed from view as the premises are impressed upon the keys. He also had designs made by means of which the same operations could be accomplished by means of electro-magnets.

Nothing whatever is known of the "hotel annunciator" machine, but a circuit design for its electromagnetically operated version was recently found among Marquand's papers by Professor Alonzo Church, of Princeton's mathematics department. (A photostat of Marquand's circuit diagram is reproduced in Wolfe Mays's article, "First Circuit for an Electrical Logic Machine," *Science*, Vol. 118, Sept. 4, 1953, p. 281; and the diagram has been analyzed in detail by George W. Patterson, an electrical engineer, in "The First Electric Computer, a Magnetological Analysis," *Journal of the Franklin Institute*, Vol. 270, August, 1960, pp. 130–137. This is probably the first circuit design ever drawn for an electrically operated logic machine, though there is no evidence that the machine was ever actually built. Dr. Mays gives 1885 as the probable date the design was drawn. The wiring diagram is of no special interest, since it merely provides an electrical method by which the keys of Marquand's machine can turn the pointers. Had small light bulbs been available at the time, Marquand would undoubtedly have used them instead of his electromagnetically operated pointers.[2]

Mention also should be made of another logic device invented by Marquand and described in his article "A Machine for Producing Syllogistic Variations," Johns Hopkins University *Studies in Logic*, edited by Charles Peirce, 1883, p. 12. (A paper by Marquand on "The Logic of the Epicureans" also appears in this volume.) By turning a crank, the face of this machine exhibits in turn the eight different forms in which a syllogism can be expressed, assuming that each statement of the syllogism has two "contraposed" forms (e.g., "All *A* is *B*" or "All not-*B* is not-*A*). The device would have delighted Ramon Lull, for it is merely an elaboration of his concentric rotating circles. By placing six rollers together in such a way that, when one was cranked, all of them would turn, the machine automatically runs through a Lullian table of exhaustive combinations for three statements, each of which is expressible in two forms. As Marquand points out, the same device can be used for other combinatorial purposes such as running through Jevons's logical alphabet for three terms.

The next advance in machines of the Jevons type seems to have been made by an Englishman named Charles P. R. Macaulay, about whom I have been able to learn nothing. In 1910, when he was living in Chicago, he applied for an American patent on a four-term logic machine. It was issued in 1913 as Patent 1,079,504 (obtainable for 25 cents from the U.S. Patent Office, Washington, D.C.). The machine combines, it seems to me, the best features of both Jevons's and Marquand's machines, with other features that make for an extremely compact and easily operated device. It is a small boxlike structure with three rows of windows through which various combinations of terms may be seen. Tilting the box in either of two directions causes interior rods to slide back and forth. Eight projecting pins on the left side of the box stand for the four terms and their negations. Pressing these pins causes the rods inside to lock in various positions so that, when the box is tilted, desired combinations can be brought into view. Consistent combinations appear in the upper row of windows, inconsistent combinations in the lower row. In the center row one can temporarily place combinations involved in particular ("some") propositions, a distinct improvement over both the Jevons and Marquand machines.

In his lengthy description of the machine, Macaulay explicitly points out its use for propositional logic. "The letters," he writes, "may be made to denote not only things, but also qualities, the truth of propositions, or any circumstances whatever." To illustrate, Macaulay poses the following problem: "Four hunters, *A, B, C* and *D,* occupied a camp in different ways for seven days. (1) On days when *A* hunted, *B* did not. (2) On days when *B* hunted, *D* also hunted, but *C* did not. (3) On days when *D* hunted, *A* or *B* hunted. How did they dispose themselves during the week? On how many days did *D* hunt and with whom?" As an interesting exercise, the reader may wish to solve this problem by Jevons's logical alphabet, or by one of the diagrammatic methods described earlier.

Although traditional syllogisms can be tested on machines of the Jevons type, the handling is, as we have seen, rather awkward. Since

114

Stanhope invented his demonstrator a number of other contrivances have been designed specifically for syllogisms, but none more fantastic than one developed by Annibale Pastore (b. 1868), professor of philosophy at the University of Genoa, Italy, and author of several books including one on *The Philosophy of Lenin*. The device, which strongly resembles a Rube Goldberg contraption, was constructed in 1903 with the aid of physics professor Antonio Garbasso. It is explained in preposterous detail in Pastore's work *Logica Formale, dedotta della considerazione di modelli meccanici (Formal Logic Deduced from the Consideration of Mechanical Models)*, published in Turin, 1906.[3]

Pastore's machine is an attempt to translate the structure of syllogistic reasoning into physical movement somewhat in the manner of an analogue computer. It consists essentially of a triangular arrangement of three groups of wheels representing the subject, predicate, and middle terms, and a complicated arrangement of differential gears, screws, weighted pendulums, and endless belts that join the wheels in a manner appropriate to the syllogism under consideration. Each group of wheels consists of one large wheel, representing "all" of its class, and two smaller wheels representing "some" of the same class. A universal affirmative proposition (All *A* is *B*) is indicated by running a belt from the large wheel of *A* to a small wheel of *B* so that, when *A* is turned, *B* will turn in the same direction. When two connected wheels rotate in opposite directions, a negative relation is indicated. Thus the universal negative (No *A* is *B*) is obtained by joining the large wheels of *A* and *B* with a belt that crosses itself between the wheels. An uncrossed belt joining two

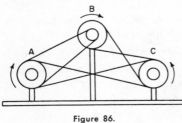

Figure 86.

small wheels is the particular positive (Some *A* is *B*) and a crossed belt from a small wheel to a large one is the particular negative (Some *A* is not *B*). Thus the syllogism: All *A* is *B*, No *B* is *C*, No *A* is *C*, would have belts connecting the wheels as shown in Figure 86.

If the belts represent a valid syllogism, cranking wheel *A* will cause all three wheels to rotate smoothly. If the wheels refuse to rotate, the syllogism is not valid. The device is designed primarily as a mechanical model of syllogistic inference rather than a machine for disclosing the valid conclusions of a given pair of premises.

To make the wheels respond properly to the structure indicated by the belts, a complicated arrangement of differential gears is necessary. For example, when a large wheel rotates, it must move the two smaller wheels on the same axle (since if all *A* is *B*, then some *A* must be *B*), but when a small wheel rotates, the large wheel must remain stationary (since if some *A* is *B*, we know nothing about all of *A*). But this is not all. To extend the power of the machine beyond the bounds of the traditional syllogism, Mr. Pastore added a second small wheel to each axle so that "some *A* is *B*" and "some *A* is not *B*" could be represented simultaneously by permitting the two small wheels of *A* to rotate in opposite directions while the large wheel remained motionless (since we know nothing about all of *A*).

A chart at the back of Pastore's book shows the belt connections for 256 possible combinations of syllogistic premises and conclusions. Of the 256, Pastore finds 32 valid syllogisms instead of the usual 24. This increased number is due to the fact that the machine recognizes as valid such syllogisms as: Some *A* is *B*, Some *B* is *C*, Some *A* is *C*, provided that the "some" is regarded as the *same* "some" in both premises. Of the 24 traditionally valid syllogisms, a few which require the assumption of non-empty classes are not validated by the machine.

As clumsy as Pastore's contrivance is, it does suggest that there are probably a wide variety of ways in which formal logic can be translated into simple mechanical phenomena.[4] There is no reason why, for example, rotating wheels cannot be used to express the propositional calculus. Each term would be represented by a wheel that rotated in one direction if the term were true, in the opposite direction if false. The relation of equivalence would be fed to the machine by setting gears so that, if either of two wheels were turned, the other wheel would turn in the same direction. "*A* implies *B*" would require that, when wheel *A* turned in a true direction, *B* would turn the same way, and when *B* turned in a false direction, *A* would turn likewise; but otherwise, turning either wheel would have no effect on the other. In similar fashion, the other binary relations could be expressed by suitable gear arrangements. If such a machine were fed a set of consistent premises, the wheels should all

116

rotate in directions indicating the truth or falsity of the various terms. Indeterminate terms would be revealed by stationary wheels. Contradictions would result in locked wheels, and theorems would be disclosed by wheels that all rotated in a true direction only, regardless of which wheel was turned. Simple arithmetical calculating machines have been based on rotating disks (including one invented by Lord Stanhope), but whether this approach would result in a logic machine efficient enough to be of interest is an open question.

All the mechanical devices considered thus far, including Jevons's machine, are decidedly inferior in speed and power to the electric machines constructed in recent years. But before turning to this last and most exciting phase of our history, it remains to glance briefly at a grid principle by which cards can be superimposed to arrive at solutions of elementary logic problems.

References

1. The Mitchell to whom Peirce refers is one of his students, Prof. O. H. Mitchell, whose influential paper "On a New Algebra of Logic" appeared in the Johns Hopkins University *Studies in Logic,* edited by Peirce in 1883.

2. Not until the early 1970s did a letter come to light that Peirce had sent Marquand in 1886. After expressing belief that Marquand's machine could be improved to handle "very difficult problems," Peirce added: "I think electricity would be the best thing to rely on." Peirce then actually sketched circuits for both conjunction and disjunction, the first known effort to apply Boolean algebra to the design of switching circuits! See "Logic, Biology and Automata—Some Historical Reflections," by Arthur W. Burks, *International Journal of Man-Machine Studies,* Vol. 7, 1975, pp. 297–312.

3. Pastore's book is reviewed at length by André Lalande in Vol. 63, 1907, pp. 268 ff., of the *Revue philosophique de la France et de l'etranger.* Lalande is sharply critical of Pastore's confused belief that his machine provides a genuine "experimental" approach to formal logic.

4. There is a sense in which all mechanical phenomena are expressive of logical relations. A lever with a fulcrum at one end will lift a weight at its center "if and only if" the other end is raised. But if the fulcrum is at the center, a weight on either end is raised only when the other end is lowered, a precise analogue of exclusive disjunction. A typewriter contains hundreds of working parts that can be considered expressions of "and," "or," "if, then," and other logical relations. This is what Peirce had in mind when he wrote, ". . . every machine is a reasoning machine, in so much as there are certain relations between its parts, which relations involve other relations that were not expressly intended. A piece of apparatus for performing a physical or chemical experiment is also a reasoning machine, with this difference, that it does not depend on the laws of the human mind, but on the objective reason embodied in the laws of nature. Accordingly, it is no figure of speech to say that the alembics and cucurbits of the chemist are instruments of thought, or logical machines." (Charles Peirce, "Logical Machines," *American Journal of Psychology,* Vol. 1, November, 1887).

7: Window Cards

Both the Stanhope demonstrator and the Pastore machine operate along mechanical lines that are in some ways analogous to the formal structure of syllogistic inference. If one is unconcerned with such analogy, desiring only a device that will produce the required conclusion from any pair of premises, then it is possible to invent a wide variety of simple gadgets for such purpose. Perhaps the simplest is a set of cards, one for each possible premise, with openings or "windows" cut on the cards in such a way that, when one card is placed on top of another, the valid conclusion, if any, will be revealed through one of the windows. When I designed a set of such cards for my article on "Logic Machines" (*Scientific American*, March, 1952) I thought I was certainly the first person ever to waste time on such a curious project. Later I discovered that the idea was at least seventy years old! Jevons, in his *Studies in Deductive Logic*, Chapter XI, describes a set of syllogistic window cards invented by a Mr. Henry Cunynghame. These cards are reproduced in Figure 87.

The working of Cunynghame's cards is easily explained. The premises appear at the top of each card. Major premises (in classical logic the major premise relates the middle term M to the predicate P of the conclusion) are at the top of eight cards; minor premises (relating the middle term M to the subject S of the conclusion) are at the top of the remaining eight. If we pick any major card, place a minor card on top, then all valid conclusions (if any) will

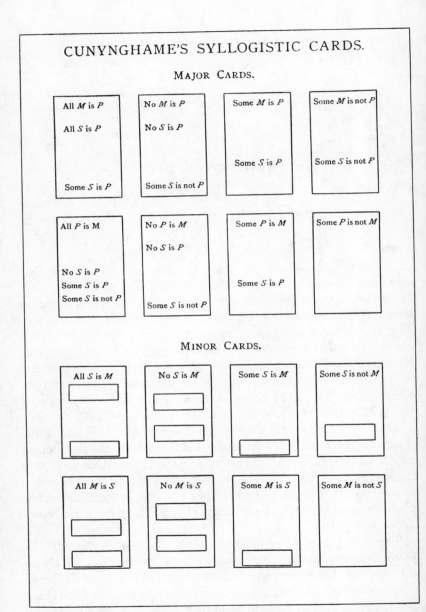

Figure 87. Grid cards for syllogisms. (From *Studies in Deductive Logic*, 1884, by William S. Jevons.)

appear in the window or windows of the upper card. Cunynghame applied the same principle to a metal device consisting of a hollow cylinder, with windows, that could be rotated around an inner solid cylinder. Jevons gives a brief description of it in the chapter just cited. A third device using the grid principle was presented by Cunynghame to the Science Museum, South Kensington, London, in 1885 but has not been on exhibition there for many years. This is simply a flat projection of the cylindrical model; a kind of circular slide rule. One cardboard disk, with slotted windows, turns upon a larger cardboard disk. Major premises appear on the circumference of the larger circle, minor premises on the circumference of the smaller one. When two premises are brought together, the conclusions, if any, appear in the openings below the minor premise. In a sense, it is a Lullian device, for the circles provide all possible combinations of premises with the additional feature of pointing out which combinations yield valid conclusions and what those conclusions are.[1]

None of these variations, however, exhibits in its construction or operation anything that resembles the formal structure of class logic. If you arbitrarily assume that certain invalid syllogisms are valid, and certain valid ones not, only a few alterations in the devices are necessary in order to obtain the new answers as readily as the old. For this reason, they have less logical interest than devices which may be clumsier to use, but which operate by principles analogous to the structure they are designed to analyze.

My set of cards for the *Scientific American* article is reproduced in Figure 88. In some respects these cards are simpler than Cunynghame's, in other ways more elaborate. Since the statement "No *A* is *B*" means the same thing as "No *B* is *A*," and similarly, "Some *A* is *B*" is the same as "Some *B* is *A*," I combined these equivalent statements on the same card. (Of course Cunynghame could have done the same, thus reducing the number of his cards from sixteen to twelve.) By adding an additional "conclusion card" with four windows for the four possible conclusions, I was able to prepare the premise cards so that it does not matter which card is put on top of the other. The two cards are simply placed together, the conclusion card put on top, and any window that shows solid black indicates a valid conclusion.

To make this clearer, suppose we wish to determine if the fol-

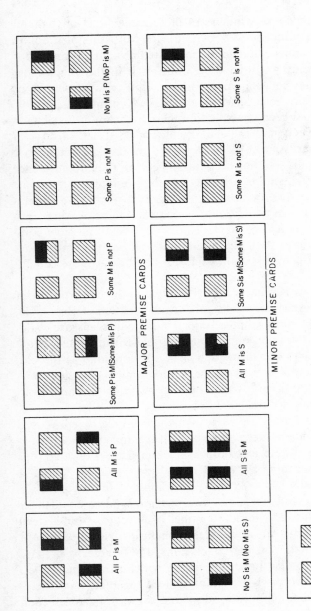

Figure 88. Grid cards for syllogisms. Areas shaded with slanting lines are cut out to make openings. (From *Scientific American*, March, 1952.)

lowing syllogism, voiced by the Patchwork Girl in L. Frank Baum's *The Lost Princess of Oz*, is valid:

> Somebody in Oz stole Ozma.
> Only wicked people steal.
> Therefore, someone in Oz is wicked.

We can state the conclusion more formally as "Some of the people in Oz are wicked people." "People in Oz" is therefore our subject (*S*), and "wicked people" the predicate (*P*). The premise containing *P* is traditionally regarded as the major premise. In this case it can be stated, "All people who steal are wicked people." The minor premise, containing *S*, may be phrased, "Some of the people in Oz are people who steal."

Our syllogism is, therefore, of the mood *IAI* (*Dimaris*) in the first figure:

> All *M* is *P*
> Some *S* is *M*
> Some *S* is *P*

To test this, we find the two premise cards and place them together, either above the other. When we cover them with the conclusion card we find that the window for "Some *S* is *P*" is solid black. This confirms the syllogism and indicates that the Patchwork Girl was not so scatterbrained as her behavior and conversation often suggested.

A more elaborate set of syllogism cards is pictured in Figure 89. To test a syllogism with them, pick out the desired major-premise card, put on top of it the desired minor-premise card, and on top of both, the desired conclusion card. If the syllogism is valid, the letter "T" will appear in one of the windows. If the syllogism is invalid, whatever formal fallacies are involved will appear along the right margin of the cards.

Grid cards can also be designed to operate on the same basis as the Venn diagrams (or Jevons's logical alphabet). They are awkward to use on syllogisms, but work fairly well with elementary problems in the propositional or truth-value calculus. If there are more than three terms, however, the number of cards required is so large that they serve no useful purpose.

Figure 90 shows a set of triangular-shaped cards of this type for

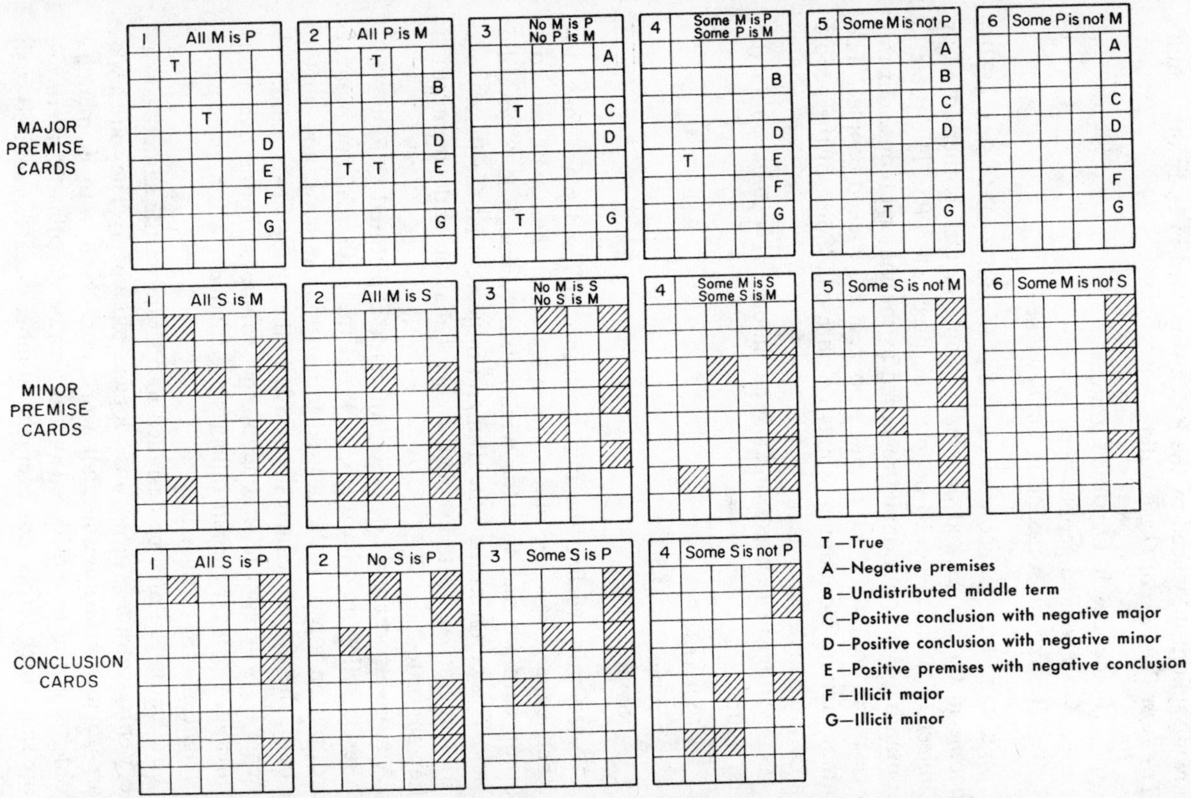

Figure 89. Grid cards that disclose formal fallacies of invalid syllogisms. Shaded areas cut out.

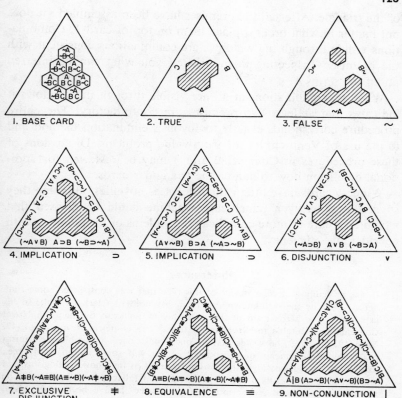

Figure 90. Triangular grid cards for propositional logic. Shaded areas are cut out.

handling up to three terms in the propositional calculus. Premises must be no more complicated than a binary relation or the assertion of truth or falsity for a single term. Only nine cards are shown in the illustration, but you should have on hand several duplicates of each card except the first one, since the same card may be required for more than one premise.

Cards 2 and 3 assert the truth value of a single term. Cards 4 through 9 are for binary relations. The basic form of the relation is shown on the edge, with less commonly encountered equivalent statements lettered on the same edge inside of parentheses. To solve a problem, pick out the required card for each premise, turning the card so that the premise appears on the bottom edge or base of the triangle. After all the premises have been assembled (it does not matter in what order), place them on top of card 1. Combinations visible through the windows are combinations consistent with the premises. Inspecting them will tell you what can be inferred about the terms.[2]

When no combinations at all are visible through the windows it indicates that at least two premises are contradictory. The entire procedure corresponds exactly to Jevons's elimination method and to the use of Venn circles for truth-value problems. Discussions of these procedures in Chapters 2 and 3 may be reviewed for additional details on how to handle the triangular cards.

Window cards have little value except as novelties, although they suggest how easily a punch-card machine could be devised that would take care of more complicated problems of formal logic with considerable efficiency.

References

1. It was probably a circular device of this type that was constructed some time before 1935 by the well-known American psychologist Clark L. Hull. In his article on "The Mechanism of the Assembly of Behavior Segments in Novel Combinations Suitable for Problem Solution," *Psychological Review,* Vol. 42, May, 1935, p. 219, he writes that he once constructed a "simple mechanism of sliding disk-segments of sheet-metal which will solve automatically, i.e., exhibit the conclusions logically flowing from all of the known syllogisms and which will automatically detect all of the formal fallacies." Hull adds that he has not yet published a description of the device. I have been unsuccessful in attempts to learn more about its construction.

2. A slightly modified set of these cards is described in the second edition of *Mathematical Models,* by H. Martyn Cundy and A. P. Rollett, 1961, pp. 256–258. Their book also shows how punched cards, with holes and slots to permit sorting by inserted rods, will solve problems in Boolean algebra. I had written about such cards in my *Scientific American* column for December 1960; an article that became the first chapter of my *New Mathematical Diversions from Scientific American* (1966).

   Caxton C. Foster, a computer scientist at the University of Massachusetts, some years ago designed an ingenious set of syllogism cards that combines a window with the punched-cards principle. Eight cards, each with twelve holes or slots on the right, fit inside a slightly wider envelope. The envelope has corresponding holes on the right and a window on the left. Paper fasteners are put through the two holes that correspond to the major and minor premises. The envelope is tilted to the left and shaken. If there is a valid conclusion, the proper card shifts leftward and the conclusion appears in the window.

   An improved version of my grid cards for showing syllogistic fallacies appears in Chapter 4 of *Testing for Truth,* by Richard H. Lampkin. The book was published by the author in 1962 to be used as the text for a course in general education which he was then teaching at the State University of New York at Buffalo.

8:   Early Electrical Machines

The term Boolean algebra is now applied to an uninterpreted formal system that is the simplest, most elementary level of modern logic. Actually, we should speak in the plural, Boolean algebras, because the system can be axiomized in many ways. Once formalized, it can be given two essentially different kinds of interpretation. It can be interpreted abstractly, within pure logic or mathematics, or realistically by applying it to some aspect of the physical world.

Boole interpreted his system abstractly as the algebra of classes, using 1 for the universal class (the class of all classes being considered), 0 for the null or empty class, letters for classes and their members, + for the exclusive "or," × for conjunction ("and"), and = for identity. The minus sign stood for the removal of one class from another. Thus the complement of x was expressed by $x - 1$, meaning the class that resulted when you took x from the universal class. Boole had no symbol for class inclusion, but he could express it in various ways, such as $a \times b = a$, meaning that the class consisting of both a and b is identical with all of a.

Boole's clumsy notation is no longer used, but with new symbols and rules, the formal structure of his system has two abstract interpretations of great contemporary interest. One is its interpretation in elementary finite set theory, and the other, as we have seen, is the propositional calculus in which letters stand for propositions which must be true or false. Boole himself pointed out that if 1 were taken to mean true, and 0 to mean false, his algebra could be applied to statements that are true or false, but it was left to Boole's successors to carry out this interpretation. The chart in Figure 91 displays the commonly used symbols for these two modern interpretations of Boole's algebra. On the right of the chart I have continued our practice of using the dot for conjunction, though in recent years an inverted ∨ has become a widely used symbol for "and."

126

Boolean Set Algebra	Propositional Calculus
U (UNIVERSAL SET)	T (TRUE)
Φ (NULL SET)	F (FALSE)
$a,b,c,...$ (SETS, SUBSETS, ELEMENTS)	$p,q,r,...$ (PROPOSITIONS)
$a \cup b$ (UNION: ALL OF a AND b)	$p \vee q$ (DISJUNCTION: EITHER p ALONE OR q ALONE, OR BOTH, ARE TRUE)
$a \cap b$ (INTERSECTION: WHAT a AND b HAVE IN COMMON)	$p \cdot q$ (CONJUNCTION; BOTH p AND q ARE TRUE)
$a = b$ (IDENTITY: a AND b ARE THE SAME SET.)	$p \equiv q$ (EQUIVALENCE: IF AND ONLY IF p IS TRUE, THEN q IS TRUE.)
a' (COMPLEMENT: ALL OF U THAT IS NOT a)	$\sim p$ (NEGATION: p IS FALSE.)
$a \in b$ (INCLUSION: a IS A MEMBER OF b.)	$p \supset$ (IMPLICATION: IF p IS TRUE, q IS TRUE.)

Figure 91. Corresponding symbols in two interpretations of Boolean algebra.

There are many other ways to give purely mathematical interpretations to Boolean algebra. It can be viewed as an abstract algebraic structure called a ring, or as a special type of another structure called a lattice. It can be given interpretations in combinatorial theory, information theory, graph theory, matrix theory, and metamathematical theories of formal deductive systems.

There is one curious interpretation in number theory in which the elements of a Boolean algebra are the 2^n positive integers formed by all the multiples of a set of distinct primes, with 1 added to the set. For example, take the three lowest primes: 2, 3, 5. Their multiples and 1 produce the following $2^3 = 8$ numbers: 1, 2, 3, 5, 6, 10, 15, 30. These are the factors of 30. Call 30 the universal set, and 1 the null set. Union is taken to mean the least common multiple of any pair of factors. Intersection of a pair is taken to be their greatest common divisor. Inclusion is the relation "is a factor of." The complement of a number a is $30/a$. With these interpretations, we have a consistent Boolean structure! Every theorem of Boolean set theory has its counterpart in this system based on the factors of 30.

As an exercise, substitute any two factors for a and b in a statement of De Morgan's two laws and you will find that the laws hold. For another exercise, try manipulating the Boolean algebra based on 1, 2, 3, 5, 6, 7, 10, 14, 15, 21, 30, 35, 43, 70, 105, 210. These are the $2^4 = 16$ factors of 210, obtained from the multiples of the four lowest primes: 2, 3, 5, 7, with 1 added.[1]

Among real-world applications of Boolean algebra, the most important is to systems in which energy of any sort is transmitted through a network of channels, with devices that can turn the energy on or off, and switch it from one channel to another. In the language of the propositional calculus, "true" means the energy is moving through a specified part of the network, "false" means it is not. The switching devices correspond to the binary relations, or "connectives," as they are now called.

The energy can be a flowing gas or liquid, as in modern fluid control systems (see "Fluid Control Devices," by Stanley W. Angrist, in *Scientific American,* December, 1964). It can be light beams. It can be mechanical energy transmitted by wheels, levers, pulleys, and other devices. It can even be sound waves or odors. If inhabitants of some other planet have a sense of smell as highly developed as our eyesight, they could be using computers made of odors transmitted along tubes to sniff outlets.

The energy can take the form of rolling spheres, as in several computer-like toys recently on the market: Dr. Nim, Think-a-Dot, and Digi-Comp II. Martha R. O'Kennon, a computer scientist at the University of Tennesee, Knoxville, has invented an ingenious set of what she calls Boolean cubes. They are made of plexiglass, with openings at top and bottom, and contain simple flip-flop switches. The cubes are notched so they can be piled up in various ways to model statements in Boolean algebra. Problems are solved and theorems proved by dropping marbles through them.[2]

Of course the fastest, cheapest, most reliable way of modeling Boolean algebra, as it is for calculating in mathematics, is by the movement of electricity along wires. (Calculating by laser-beam circuitry is a good possibility, but still far in the future.) As we have seen in Chapter 6, as early as 1886 Charles Peirce had grasped the ease with which binary relations in Boolean algebra could be modeled by electrical switching circuits, and his former student John Marquand actually designed an electric logic machine, although it was never constructed.

So far as I have been able to discover, the first electric logic machine actually made was a syllogism-solving device designed by Benjamin Burack, a psychologist at Roosevelt College in Chicago. He built his machine in 1936, but did not publish a description until his article "An Electrical Logic Machine" appeared in *Science,* Vol. 109, June 17, 1949, p. 610.

Burack's machine is designed to test all syllogisms, including hypothetical and disjunctive forms, and also to test the conversion

128

and obversion of propositions. To facilitate carrying, it was constructed inside a small suitcase (Figure 92). The lower part of this

case contains thin plywood blocks lettered to represent various class propositions. To test a syllogism, the three required blocks are selected and placed in three spaces on the left side of the panel that fills the upper half of the suitcase. Metal contact areas on the backs of the blocks establish electrical connections between contact points on the panel so that, if the syllogism is invalid, one or more bulbs light up on the right side of the panel. The bulbs are labeled to indicate seven basic fallacies of the categorical syllogism, three fallacies for the hypothetical, one for the disjunctive,

Figure 92. Burack's syllogism machine.

one for false conversion, and one for false obversion. An additional bulb indicates that the electric current (either battery or line) has been established.

Since Burak first exhibited his machine, so many other types of electrical syllogism machines have been built, most of them by university students interested in logic and cybernetics, that it would be a difficult task to gather details about even a small portion of them. It is possible today to build simple syllogism machines with the parts of computer kits currently on sale for children or with the "logic breadboards" now widely used for the teaching of computer logic designs.

None of these syllogism machines has a network that corresponds in any formal way with the structure of class logic. They are like the window cards of the previous chapter, using electrical connections, instead of the presence or absence of openings, to screen off invalid conclusions and transmit valid ones. When, however, we turn to the electrical machines that have been designed for the propositional calculus we enter an altogether different domain. Here we find a striking analogy between the wire networks and the formal structure of the logic that the networks manipulate.

The isomorphism between switching circuits and Boolean algebra was first suggested by Peirce in his unpublished letter to Marquand. In 1910 Paul Ehrenfest made a similar suggestion in a Russian journal when he reviewed Couterat's *Algébra logiki*. Details were worked out in 1934–1935 by the Russian physicist V. I. Sestakov, but not published until 1941. Independently, the same views were set forth in 1936 in a Japanese journal by Aikira Nakasima and Masao Hanzawa, as reported in the *Journal of Symbolic Logic*, Vol. 18, December, 1953, p. 345.

The greatest stimulus to work along these lines was Claude E. Shannon's historic article, "A Symbolic Analysis of Relay and Switching Circuits," in the *Transactions of the American Institute of Electrical Engineers,* Vol. 57, December, 1938, p. 713 ff. The paper was based on Shannon's master's thesis at the Massachusetts Institute of Technology. In it Shannon explained in detail how relay and switching circuits can be expressed by equations which can be manipulated by Boolean algebra. True and false correspond to the open and closed states of a circuit, and the binary connectives are modeled by various kinds of switches. Figure 93 shows three simple switching circuits that model the relations of "and," the inclusive "or," and the exclusive "or." If you have two wall switches in your house that control a single light, you are using a circuit that is a trivial logic machine based on the relation of nonequivalence!

Shannon's paper laid the groundwork for both the construction of special-purpose truth-value electric machines and for new methods by which electrical circuits can be designed and simplified. Unnecessarily complex circuits can be translated into the propositional calculus, the statement simplified, then translated back to a simpler circuit. Or a new circuit can be devised by stating its desired characteristic in the simplest possible logic form, then converting the statement to a circuit. Today the networks of all computers, from giants to pocket-sized, are drawn with labels at each switch point that indicate the logical nature of the switch. These symbols (sometimes called diagrams, but only in the sense of labels) are now fairly standardized around the world. Figure 94 shows what some of them look like, with their names and their meaning as expressed in the notation we have been using.

Since Shannon's pioneering paper, there has been an explosive development in the application of logic to switching circuit design, with so many hundreds of important papers that it would be hopeless to cite even a selection. It is a striking instance of how once again, in

"And" Circuit: bulb lights only
if both **a** and **b** are closed.

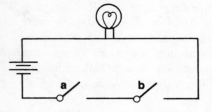

Inclusive "or" Circuit: bulb lights only
if **a** or **b** or both are closed.

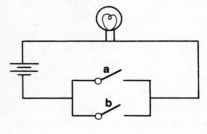

Exclusive "or" Circuit: bulb lights only
if **a** or **b**, but *not* both, is lowered.

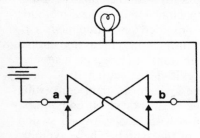

Figure 93. Circuits for three binary relations.

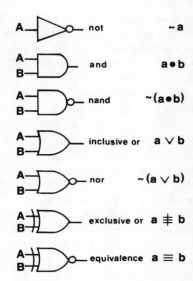

not	~a	
and	a•b	
nand	~(a•b)	
inclusive or	a ∨ b	
nor	~(a ∨ b)	
exclusive or	a ≢ b	
equivalence	a ≡ b	

Figure 94. Logic symbols for switches in
electrical circuitry.

the history of science and technology, an abstract subject pursued
for its own sake, with no apparent practical application, has unex-
pectedly turned out to be enormously useful. The world has now
plunged into a new industrial revolution of awesome scope, with
computers invading almost every aspect of technology. The complex, sophisticated circuitry of these machines was made possible by
the labors of early logicians who had no inkling of the applications to

which their efforts would be put. Today their work is of growing importance in increasing the speed, power, and dependability of computers and computer-controlled machines.

Our next chapter will say more about this revolution, but first let us glance at some of the primitive, now obsolete, electrical logic machines that were built after World War II and examine their use before they proved to be unnecessary because what they did could be done more easily by general-purpose digital computers. These special-purpose machines are now curiosities, as useless as slide rules and the old electrical adding machines. Nevertheless, they have enough historical interest to justify a quick look at them.

The first electrical machine designed solely for propositional logic was built in 1947 by two undergraduates at Harvard, William Burkhart and Theodore A. Kalin. They had been taking a course in symbolic logic with Professor Willard V. Quine and they had chanced upon Shannon's paper on the relation of such logic to switching circuits. Weary of solving problems by laborious paper and pencil methods, and unaware of any previous logic machines, they decided to build an electrical device that would do their homework automatically. The result, at a cost of about $150 for the materials, was a small machine—now known as the Kalin-Burkhart machine— capable of handling problems involving up to twelve terms in the propositional calculus. The machine was first described in Edmund C. Berkeley's *Giant Brains* (1949) from which the following brief account is taken.

Premises are fed to the Kalin-Burkhart machine by setting switches which establish a circuit pattern isomorphic with the logical structure of the combined premises. The machine then scans the entire truth table for this structure, taking the lines one at a time at a rate of about one-half second per line. Each line is indicated on the face of the machine by the pattern of lights in a row of twelve red bulbs that correspond to the twelve terms. A glowing bulb indicates that the term is true. A yellow bulb lights whenever a row of the truth table is valid, does not light when the row is false. Thus by watching the machine and stopping it whenever a truth-table line is valid, one can copy down the pattern of true and false terms as indicated by the twelve red bulbs. The machine can also be set to stop automatically when the yellow light is on, but must be started again manually. It is interesting to note that when certain types of paradoxes are fed to the Kalin-Burkhart machine it goes into an oscillating phase, switching rapidly back and forth from true to false. In a letter to Burkhart in 1947 Kalin described one such example and concluded, "This may be a version of Russell's paradox. Anyway, it makes a hell of a racket."

It should be apparent that the Kalin-Burkhart machine is in a sense simply an electrical version of Jevons's logical piano. Its great superiority over Jevons's device is its power to handle many more terms, a power derived chiefly from the fact that instead of showing valid lines of a truth table simultaneously (creating an enormous space problem if many terms are involved), it takes the lines in a serial time sequence. This also may be considered a weakness in the machine, for it requires an operator to copy down the lines as they appear. This could be easily overcome, however, by adding to the machine an automatic recording mechanism.

The first electrical logic machine built in England, the Ferranti logical computer, was one that handled three terms only in the propositional calculus. Like the Kalin-Burkhart computer it operated by producing truth tables although its construction, in 1949, was on a different basis and made without knowledge of the work of Burkhart and Kalin. The Ferranti machine was jointly devised by Dr. Wolfe Mays, senior lecturer in philosophy at the University of Manchester, where Jevons himself had once taught, and D. G. Prinz of Ferranti, Ltd., Manchester. It was first described in a brief paper by Mays and Prinz, "A Relay Machine for the Demonstration of Symbolic Logic," *Nature*, Vol. 165, Feb. 4, 1950, p. 197. Plans for a more elaborate multivariable machine were announced by Dr. Mays ("Note on the Exhibition of Logical Machines," *Mind*, Vol. 60, April, 1951, p. 262), but the machine was never completed.

After 1949 scores of other electrical logic machines were built in various parts of the world, only a few of which were announced or described in journals. The following is a partial list of references in English to some of these machines.

1. A three-term electronic device built at the National Physical Laboratory, Pretoria, South Africa, that exhibits its solutions on an oscilloscope screen. ("Venn Diagram Analogue Computer," by Alva Izak Archer, *Nature*, Vol. 166, Nov. 11, 1950, and his article of the same title, *South African Journal of Science,* Vol. 47, 1950, p. 133.) John von Neumann had been the first to explain how two high frequency oscillators, 180 degrees out of phase, could be used to indicate binary digits in a logic machine. Apparently the Pretoria device was based on this scheme.

2. A seven-term machine built in 1950 at the Edinburgh laboratory of Ferranti, Ltd., along lines similar to the Kalin-Burkhart computer, though constructed like the previous Ferranti machine

without knowledge of the earlier American device. Pressing a button labeled "Think" starts the machine scanning a truth table for the combined premises fed to the machine. The machine stops on all "true" lines to permit copying, then starts scanning again when the "Think" button is pressed. ("Mechanized Reasoning: Logical Computers and Their Design," by D. M. McCallum and J. B. Smith, *Electronic Engineering,* Vol. 23, April, 1951.)

3. A four-term machine built in 1951 by Robert W. Marks, New York, N.Y., and first announced in my article, "Logic Machines," *Scientific American,* March, 1952. To add a touch of whimsy, Marks attached a wire recorder and loud-speaker to his device so that it delivered its answers in a deep, impressive voice. For example, if a tested theorem proved to be false, the machine would say, "My name is Leibnitz Boole De Morgan Quine. I am nothing but a complicated and slightly neurotic robot, but it gives me great pleasure to announce that your statement is absolutely false."

4. A "feedback logical computer" for four terms. By using a feedback principle the machine is able to scan a problem in such a way that it can find *one* answer (that is, one "true" line of a combined truth table) without running through an entire truth table until it encounters one. If all possible answers are desired, the principle is of no value, but there are certain complex problems in which only a single answer is demanded. In such cases the machine cuts down the scanning time required to find this answer. The device was built in 1951 at the Edinburgh laboratory of Ferranti, Ltd. ("Feedback Logical Computers," by D. M. McCallum and J. B. Smith, *Electronic Engineering,* Vol. 23, December, 1951.)

5. A ten-term "truth-function evaluator" constructed at the Burroughs Research Center, Paoli, Pennsylvania. It employs a logical notation proposed by Jan Lukasiewicz in which all parentheses are eliminated by placing the variables and connectives in order from left to right according to the conventions of the notation. This has certain mechanical advantages. It is interesting to note that the idea of using the Lukasiewicz notation had occurred to Kalin as early as 1947. In a letter to Burkhart, August 13, 1947, he discussed this at some length, expressing his opinion that "if there's ever a market for logic machines, I'll bet this is the most practical way to set up any useful (i.e., complicated) problem." ("An Analysis of a Logical Machine Using Parenthesis-free Notation," by Arthur W. Burks, Don W. Warren, and Jesse B. Wright, *Mathematical Tables and Other Aids to Computation,* Vol. 8, April, 1954, p. 53; reviewed in *Journal of Symbolic Logic,* Vol. 20, March, 1956, p. 70. See also William

134

Miehle's paper, "Burroughs Truth Function Evaluator," *Journal of the Association for Computing Machinery,* Vol. 4, April, 1957, p. 189.)

6. A relay machine handling up to eight variables in the propositional calculus, designed and built in 1952 by Melvin Earl Maron, then on the staff of IBM Engineering Research and Development Laboratory, San Jose, California. The machine was described in Maron's then confidential technical report, "A Decision Machine for the Sentential Calculus," published by the laboratory and dated March 6, 1953.

7. A five-term machine constructed in 1954 by Roger W. Holmes, a philosopher at Mount Holyoke College, South Hadley, Massachusetts (Associated Press photograph and caption, distributed to newspapers of March 8, 1954).

All the above machines, with the possible exception of the first one, were designed to run through truth tables. It is true that truth tables can be scanned very quickly if only a few terms are involved, but as the number of terms increases, the scanning time increases at an exponential rate. In the next chapter we shall see how methods have been devised which avoid scanning an entire truth table to test the validity of a theorem, but so far as I know, no special-purpose logic machines have been built which take advantage of these new algorithms.

If a special-purpose machine is designed for testing indeterminate statements (statements that are neither tautologies nor inconsistent) to determine what truth values for individual terms are uniquely determined by a given statement or set of statements, it may be possible to design a machine that would neither be forced to run through truth tables nor make long chains of deductions as in modern algorithms for testing logic statements on general-purpose computers. Such machines would be given a statement, involving a not-too-large number of terms, by setting switches or inserting components that would transform the machine's circuitry into a network in some way isomorphic with the statement. When turned on, the machine would instantly show the exact status of each variable, perhaps with a red bulb for true, green bulb for false, and blue for indeterminate. Simultaneous lighting of a red and green bulb for a term would indicate a contradiction. If only red bulbs lit, it would indicate a theorem. I do not know if it is possible to design a special-purpose machine of this sort; at any rate, I know of no attempt to do so.

Another defect of all electrical machines that generate truth tables (it is a defect they share with their mechanical ancestors) is that they do not provide answers to logic problems in their simplest, most economic form. (We enountered this difficulty in connection with Jevons's machine.) The "answer" is usually a set of true lines from a truth table, and it takes considerable ingenuity and creative effort to arrive at a simple, condensed statement of what the machine has discovered. For example, a machine may disclose that the following two-term statement is valid: $AB \vee {\sim}AB \vee A{\sim}B$. This disjunctive chain is identical with the simpler statement $A \vee B$, but the machine is powerless to make such a reduction.

The task of "minimizing" a complex disjunctive chain of the sort formed by joining the true lines of a truth table is not easy. Early efforts to formulate procedures are given by John N. Keynes in the fourth edition of his *Studies and Exercises in Formal Logic* (1906). (One method goes back to 1892.) Some modern methods rely on charts. The most popular chart method uses what is called a Karnaugh map after Maurice Karnaugh, who based his maps on an earlier diagram called the Veitch chart, after Edward W. Veitch. Both Veitch charts and Karnaugh maps are variants of Marquand's diagram. A Karnaugh map for four terms is shown in Figure 95.

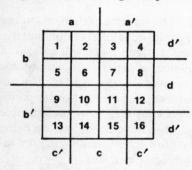

Figure 95. Karnaugh map for four variables.

Each numbered cell represents a unique combination of true-false values for the terms a, b, c, d. Karnaugh first explained how to use his maps for minimizing in "The Map Method for Synthesis of Combinational Logic Circuits," *Transactions of the American Institute of Electrical Engineers,* Vol. 72, Part 1, November, 1953, pp. 593–599. There is now a large literature on Karnaugh maps, and other geometrical and algebraic methods of minimizing logic statements and their corresponding circuitry, but no completely satisfactory systematic procedure has yet been found. Attempts have been made to use Karnaugh maps for more than four variables (some Karnaugh maps are three dimensional), but they become less efficient as the number of terms increases.

What can be done by hand can of course be done by a computer. So far as I know, the first special-purpose minimizing computer was built in 1952 by Daniel G. Bobrow, now a distinguished expert on artificial intelligence who works for Xerox. He was then a student at the Bronx High School of Science in New York. He described his machine in a privately printed manuscript titled "A Symbolic Logic Machine to Minimize Boolean Functions in Four Variables, and Application to Switching Circuits." Here again, the literature on minimizing is large, and any recent references I might cite would quickly become out of date. The new methods involve clever programs for digital computers, it no longer being useful to build special-purpose devices for this task.

The task of minimizing is complicated by the fact that what is meant by "simplest" or "most economical" circuit varies considerably with the kind of hardware involved. It is true that a circuit can be designed for any logic statement, but minimizing the length of the statement does not necessarily translate to the best circuit. The Karnaugh map technique is limited to minimizing the number of terms in a disjunctive chain, but a circuit designer may want to simplify in some other sense. He may want, for example, to minimize the number of connections, or to minimize the time it takes a current to do what it is supposed to do, and so on. Much work is now underway on the "synthesizing problem," as it is usually called by engineers, but as I said, no fully satisfactory algorithms have yet been found.

We have considered only the task of minimizing statements in the propositional calculus. When we go to the next level of complexity, the first-order predicate calculus (about which more will be said in the next chapter), the task of finding a general procedure for minimizing is hopeless. It would depend on the existence of an algorithm for deciding if any two sentences of the first-order predicate calculus are equivalent, but this is known to be an undecidable problem. Of course procedures have been developed, and are being improved, that will do a reasonably good job of minimizing for restricted portions of the first-order predicate calculus.

References

1. A proof that number sets generated in this way form a Boolean algebra will be found in *Boolean Algebra,* by Robert Louis Goodstein, Macmillan, 1963, in the answer to problem 10, p. 126.
2. On modeling calculations in arithmetic and Boolean algebra by rolling balls through channels controlled by switches, see Barry Pilton, "The Intelligent Ball Bearing," *Manifold* (published by Warwick University, Manchester, England), Spring, 1971, pp. 17–20; Benjamin Schwartz, "Mathematical Theory of Think-a-Dot, *Mathematics Magazine,* Vol. 40, September, 1967, pp. 187–193; Sidney Kravitz, "Additional Mathematical Theory of Think-a-Dot," *Journal of Recreational Mathematics,* Vol. 1, October, 1968, pp. 247–250; and John A. Beidler, "Think-a-Dot Revisited," *ibid.,* Vol. 46, May, 1973, pp. 128–136.

"And can it really think?" asked one of them.

"It can beat me at chess," said Pender.

"Really?" said the man. "That's clever of it. But perhaps chess is not such a difficult game, if you don't play it the way the professionals do."

—Lord Dunsany, *The Last Revolution*

9:   Machine Intelligence

Special-purpose electrical logic machines had a short life, roughly, the years from 1947 to 1957. There were two reasons why they disappeared. First, general-purpose digital computers had become faster, more powerful, more reliable, smaller, less costly, and more plentiful. As Bertram Raphael opens his splendid book, *The Thinking Computer* (W. H. Freeman, 1976): "In the mid-1940's the first experimental computers consisted of rooms full of equipment that cost millions of dollars, were available only to a few elite scientists, and constantly broke down. Today . . . machines with similar computational speed and precision can be purchased in any department store for about $100, fit in the palm of your hand, and work reliably for years." A single chip, smaller than a dime, now has the power of computers that once filled large rooms. If Bell Labs' new bubble memory lives up to its billing, computers will soon be even tinier and faster.

The second reason electrical logic machines vanished is that it is easy to write programs that tell a computer how to manipulate the lower levels of formal logic. Since 1960 all computer work on formal logic has been done on general-purpose computers. The public may still think of them as just big, complicated arithmetic machines, but they obviously are much more than that. As Ted Nelson likes to say, they are essentially machines that twiddle symbols. The symbols often are, of course, numbers, but they also can be such things as positions on a chess board, musical tones, words of ordinary languages, statements about medical symptoms, or a thousand other things. Formal logic, above all, consists of symbols and rules for twiddling them.

137

Programs for the propositional calculus are so easy to write that you can put them into pocket-size programmable calculators. Here is one of the earliest methods for translating the calculus into binary numbers suitable for computer twiddling—a method so simple that nobody even knows who first thought of it. Indeed, it is so simple that you can solve three-term problems in the propositional calculus with playing cards, letting face-down cards stand for the binary digit 1, face-up cards for 0.

We begin by constructing a table that will show the four possible true-false combinations for two terms, *A* and *B*, using 1 for true, 0 for false. The left-to-right order in which the combinations appear is arbitrary. Let us assume that the following order is adopted:

A	0	1	0	1
B	0	0	1	1

The relation of equivalence can now be represented by the following "designation number": 1001. This number simply tells us that the first and fourth combinations in the above table (i.e., false-false and true-true) are "true," whereas the other two combinations (true-false and false-true) are "false." (The digits in the designation number correspond of course to the presence or absence of shuttle lines in the network diagram explained in Chapter 3.) In a similar manner we can arrive at a designation number for the other binary functions:

$$A \vee B = 0 \quad 1 \quad 1 \quad 1$$
$$A \neq B = 0 \quad 1 \quad 1 \quad 0$$
$$A \mid B = 1 \quad 1 \quad 1 \quad 0$$
$$A \supset B = 1 \quad 0 \quad 1 \quad 1$$
$$B \supset A = 1 \quad 1 \quad 0 \quad 1$$

It is now possible to adjust the digital computer so that, when it is fed a series of premises that are expressed in binary numbers, it will combine these numbers and arrive at a designation number that expresses the combined premises. The "ones" in this final designation number will then tell us what lines of the final truth table are valid. In this way we can easily determine what can be inferred as to the truth or falsity of the individual terms. In fact the first Ferranti machine, designed by D. G. Prinz, operated precisely this way, handling three-term problems in just the way they would be handled by a large digital computer.

To make the process a bit clearer, suppose we wish the computer to give us the negation of a designation number. The machine has only to replace each 1 in the number by a 0 and each 0 by a 1. Thus the negation of equivalence (1001) would be 0110, which proves to be the designation number for the exclusive "or." (This process is analogous to the method of negating a function in the network diagram by removing all shuttles and drawing in the missing ones.)

If we wish the machine to give us a designation number for two functions connected by "and," it does so simply by multiplying the corresponding pairs of digits. For example, consider the following two premises:

If and only if A is true, B is true.
A is true.

What can we say about B?

As we have seen, the designation number for the first premise, which states the equivalence of A and B, is 1001. The designation number for the second statement is simply the binary number we originally assigned to A, namely, 0101. If we now multiply the corresponding pairs of digits we obtain 0001 as the designation number for the combined premises. This number tells us that only the last combination of the original truth table is true. Referring to the original table we see that in this last combination B is 1; therefore we know that B must be true.

What we are doing, of course, is simply performing in a notational way the elimination steps that we perform when we use the Venn diagrams for the propositional calculus, or Jevons's logic machine. If our premises contain a contradiction, our final designation number will consist entirely of zeros, just as all the compartments become shaded in the Venn system or all combinations vanish from the face of Jevons's machine. If the final designation number consists entirely of ones, it indicates that all lines of the final truth table are true. In other words, the statements fed to the machine constitute a law or theorem that holds regardless of how its terms vary in their truth or falsity.

The binary method can of course be extended to any number of terms, each additional term doubling the number of digits required in the basic designation numbers. Thus if we are working with three terms we must assign an eight-digit binary number to each term to represent an eight-line truth table:

A	0	1	0	1	0	1	0	1
B	0	0	1	1	0	0	1	1
C	0	0	0	0	1	1	1	1

Each binary function will also be an eight-digit number. For example, equivalence of B and C would in this case be expressed as 11000011. Premises are combined by multiplying as previously explained to obtain a final designation number which can be checked against the original table to determine what can be deduced about the truth or falsity of individual terms.

If binary relations are linked by other functions than "and," then other simple arithmetical rules will take care of them. The inclusive "or" of disjunction is handled as ordinary addition except that when 1 is added to 1 the sum is also 1. The exclusive "or" is also handled by addition, but in this case 1 plus 1 always gives 0. Equivalence is handled like the exclusive "or" except that after the results are obtained they are negated by changing every 0 to 1 and every 1 to 0.

One example should be sufficient to make clear how these relations are handled. Suppose we wish to test the statement $(A \supset B) \vee (B \supset A)$ to see if it is a tautology. The designation number for the first implication is 1011, for the second implication 1101. To connect them by the relation of inclusive disjunction we add the numbers according to the rule given above, arriving at a final designation number of 1111. This tells us that every combination (or "line" of the truth table) is true; hence the statement is a tautology.

Tautologies may be regarded as simple theorems. The line separating theorem from tautology is fuzzy, but usually a statement is called a theorem only if it is true provided certain premises are true. Of course we can connect the premises and the theorem by "ands" to form a longer statement. If the theorem is true, this long statement can be viewed as a long tautology.

Most computer work on logic is concerned with theorem proving. In the propositional calculus, this is traditionally done, as we have learned, by constructing a truth table for the sentence to be proved, then inspecting it to see if every line is true. If so, the theorem is valid. If the statement is inconsistent—that is, if it contains a contradiction (a term that can be shown to be both true and false)—then all lines of the truth table will be false. If the statement is indeterminate, its truth-table lines will mix true and false. The truth table method always works, and of course it applies to any interpretation of Boolean algebra, as well as to multivalued logics.

Unfortunately, the number of lines in a truth table for n terms is 2^n, so if the number of terms is large, it takes a long time to run through a complete table. For as few as twenty terms, $2^{20} = 1,048,576$, so the table has more than a million lines. If a sentence is not a theorem, a computer need not go through the entire table. It can be set to stop as soon as it produces a false line. But if a theorem is true, the truth-table algorithm will not establish its validity until it completes the entire table. Because this is time-consuming if there are many terms, it is desirable to have an algorithm that will prove a theorem without having to complete a truth table. Of course a logician, using his ingenuity, can usually devise a short proof of a theorem, but computer programs are still far behind human brains in doing this kind of creative thinking. Programmers need a systematic procedure guaranteed to work in all cases.

There are many such procedures. One of the best, invented by Hao Wang in 1960, can be found in Raphael's book where it is applied to a problem based on four premises: (1) The maid said she saw the butler in the living room. (2) The living room adjoins the kitchen. (3) The shot was fired in the kitchen, and could be heard in all nearby rooms. (4) The butler, who has good hearing, said he did not hear the shot.

With these premises, you are to prove the theorem: "If the maid told the truth, the butler lied." It is easy to see that the statement is true, but the task is how best to prove it by a computer program that will apply to any statement in the propositional calculus. There are thirty-two lines in the truth table for the statement to be tested. Wang's algorithm proves the theorem in twelve steps.

Another algorithm that shortcuts the truth table is a *reductio ad absurdum* method called "propositional resolution." The statement to be proved is assumed to be false, so a statement is written to express its negation. This statement is then combined with the premises to make a longer statement which the computer translates (by a standard algorithm) into what is called its "conjunctive normal" form. This is a form in which "clauses" (parenthetical expressions consisting of terms connected by "ors") are joined by "ands." The program then applies a systematic procedure, also explained in Raphael's book, which continues until it encounters a contradiction. As soon as it does, the sentence is known to be inconsistent, and the original theorem is proved. If no contradiction is encountered, the original theorem is false.

Although there are methods for proving theorems in the propositional calculus that avoid constructing entire truth tables, even the simpler problem of determining by computer whether a sentence is "satisfiable"—whether it has at least one true line of its table—is what is now called NP-complete (NP stands for nondeterministic polynomial time). Among problems decidable by computer (that is, the computer halts with a solution after a finite running time), some have been proved "intractable" in the sense that, as the values of certain parameters increase, the complexity of the problem increases at such an explosive rate that there is no hope for a general program that will solve them in a feasible amount of time. They are solvable in principle, but hopeless practically, because the running time, as the value of a parameter grows, leaps quickly to, say, a few million years. NP-complete problems—of which the "traveling salesman" problem of graph theory is the best-known example—are among the unclassified problems not yet proved intractable (though they probably are).

The work on NP-complete problems began in 1971 when Stephen A. Cook proved that the satisfiability problem (SAT for short) for the propositional calculus is NP-complete. A year later Richard M. Karp showed how to translate certain other problems into SAT. If a problem can be so translated, it joins the growing list of hundreds of NP-complete problems, all linked in such a way that if a "feasible" algorithm is found for one, it is found for all.[1]

Let us jump now from the propositional calculus to the next level of modern logic, the first-order predicate calculus. It is much more flexible; indeed, so flexible that it can handle most (though not all) of mathematics. It is enormously useful in the field of artificial intelligence (AI). For that reason, most research today on the computer manipulation of formal logic has to do with ways of proving theorems in portions of the first-order predicate calculus.

The predicate calculus (as I shall henceforth call it) uses letters for uninterpreted variables which stand for anything you like provided you can say something about them in a formal logic. They are not just true-false propositions. They can be numbers, triangles, words, states of a chess game, people, oranges, operations, and so on. The negation symbol is used, also the binary connectives of the propositional calculus. Implication is frequently eliminated by replacing $A \supset B$ with its equivalent $\sim A \vee B$. The relation of identity, symbolized by $=$, is seldom used in AI because it introduces special difficulties for computers. Relations of other sorts are permitted, such as *A* is larger (or smaller) than *B*, *A* loves (or hates) *B*, *A* is between *B* and *C*, *A* is the father (or son) of *B*, *A* precedes (follows) *B*, and so on.

There are two quantifiers:

1. The universal quantifier. This is symbolized by ∀ (an inverted *A*), and pronounced "for all." It means all the members of a specified domain.
2. The existential quantifier. This is symbolized by ∃ (an inverted *E*), and pronounced "there exists." It means that there exists at least one member of a specified domain; the "some" in the Aristotelian logic of syllogisms. The predicate calculus also permits expressions in which ∃ can mean just one, or just two, or any other number of existing objects.

The variables and their connectives, along with punctuation marks such as parentheses, are formed according to rules into what are called "wffs" (well-formed formulas) or, more informally, "strings." If every variable in a wff is quantified by either of the two quantifiers, the formula is called a sentence. If a sentence is true for all truth-value interpretations of its nonempty variables, it is a theorem.

Unlike the propositional calculus, when predicate calculus is taken in its entirety, there is no general procedure for proving all theorems. (This is known as Church's theorem, after Alonzo Church, who first proved it.) To make matters worse, when variables stand for an infinite set of objects, such as numbers, then (as Kurt Gödel first showed) there are true theorems incapable of being proved true within the system in which they occur. Some famous conjectures in mathematics may or may not be unprovable in this sense. The classic example in number theory is Fermat's last theorem. If this is Gödel-undecidable, any computer program trying to prove it would never halt. Among the many fascinating problems which have been proved undecidable in the weaker sense (that there cannot be a computer algorithm for deciding them in general), one of the simplest was constructed in 1955 by G. S. Tsentin and Dana Scott. The five symbols, *a,b,c,d,e,* are combined to form strings. There are seven rules that allow you to change a string by substitution (the two-headed arrow means the string on either side can be substituted for the string on the other side):

1. $ac \leftrightarrow ca$
2. $ad \leftrightarrow da$
3. $bc \leftrightarrow cb$
4. $bd \leftrightarrow db$
5. $adac \leftrightarrow abac$
6. $eca \leftrightarrow ae$
7. $edb \leftrightarrow be$

Can a computer program be written that will take any finite string and decide whether it is possible to alter it, by the rules, to make another specified string? The answer is no. It is an undecidable problem!

Fortunately, most of the theorems with which AI is concerned are decidable, and there are beautiful algorithms in the predicate calculus for deciding them. The most widely used procedure is called the "resolution principle" because it is an extension of the resolution method for the propositional calculus. It was invented in 1964 by John Alan Robinson, of Syracuse University, and since improved by many others. The resolution principle is too complicated to explain here in detail, but you'll find it in Raphael's book, or any other good introduction to AI such as Nils J. Nilsson's *Problem-Solving in Artificial Intelligence* (McGraw-Hill, 1971). You won't find it in most logic textbooks because it is too new.

There is a tree graph called a "binary semantic tree," which is essentially a method of displaying a complete truth table as a tree. For a sentence in the predicate calculus, the resolution method avoids examining the entire tree by negating the sentence to be proved, then analyzing the negation by constructing what is called a "refutation graph" which is usually much smaller than the binary semantic tree. If in constructing this graph it reaches a contradiction (indicated on the graph by what is called a "nil" node), then the negation is proved false, and the original theorem is thereby established. The procedure always reaches a contradiction in a finite number of steps provided the sentence being tested is inconsistent, or "unsatisfiable," as AI researchers prefer to say, and provided it consists of a finite set of clauses.

The resolution method is sort of midway between a truth-table algorithm in which no probability is involved, and the kind of inductive trial-and-error methods used by scientists when they try to solve an empirical problem. The resolution principle searches the data systematically for a proof. It is more efficient than other methods only because the probability is high that it will find such a proof more rapidly than by exhaustively examining the entire truth table.

There is now a large literature on the proving of predicate-calculus theorems by programs using the resolution principle. (Curiously, work in the Soviet Union on the predicate calculus has been in the opposite direction, toward what is usually called "natural deduction"—the deducing of valid statements from other valid statements. In this country, Woodrow W. Bledsoe, of the University of Texas, has been the leading exponent of such methods.) The principle is so efficient that a computer can now prove all the predicate-calculus theorems in *Principia Mathematica* (which took poor Russell and Whitehead years to verify) in just a few minutes.

Moreover, the principle generalizes readily to many-valued logics, to modal logics, and to many another queer logic now being investigated. A great deal of current research has to do with finding efficient theorem-proving methods in the second-order predicate calculus and logics of higher orders. There is little point in citing even the most important research papers because they are likely to be out of date in a few years. (You can keep up with this work by subscribing to the relevant journals, and by checking the volumes of an indispensable and marvelous ongoing series called *Machine Intelligence,* of which Donald Michie is the originator and editor-in-chief. Ten volumes have been published.)

One of the most active areas of current research is on the use of logic for planning computer programs, testing their correctness, and devising programs that write other programs. Eventually we should be able to tell a computer, in ordinary language, what we want it to do, and it will at once write a program for doing it. Of course logic is involved in all computer problem solving, game playing, language translation, question-and-answer programs, operations research, computer graphics, computer music, analyzing and even designing new chemical compounds, and so on, as well as in the construction of special-purpose computers such as perception machines and robots of every variety. The future is almost unimaginable as computers make their way into nearly every aspect of science, technology, and daily living.

"Machinery would have been good enough if it stayed where it was when first we got hold of it," remarks the computer scientist in Lord Dunsany's little-known novel *The Last Revolution.* "But it grows, and grows faster than us. And it's going its own way, and dragging us with it."

"What way is that?" someone asks.

"Ah, you've gone to the root of the matter. Your words should be written on gold. We don't know."

But this is a book about formal logic, not about its applications in AI. Here are two areas of future research, involving machine logic, that seem to me of special interest:

1. Probabilistic logic. This is a form of modal logic, proposed by Hans Reichenbach, in which true and false are replaced by probabilities ranging from 1 (true) to 0 (false). Its potential application to science is obvious.

2. Fuzzy logic. As in probabilistic logic, variables can take any real value from 0 to 1 inclusive, but instead of representing probabilities that a sentence may be true (such as "The next throw of this die will be 4"), they represent the degree to which a variable is in a fuzzy set. Traditional nonfuzzy sets, called "crisp sets," are sets with a value of 1.

Work on fuzzy logic was pioneered in the United States by Lotfi A. Zadeh, a computer scientist at the University of California, Berkeley. In recent years the number of papers and conferences on fuzzy logic and fuzzy set theory has grown rapidly. A periodical called *Fuzzy Sets and Systems* is published in Amsterdam. There is a similar journal in France, another in China. Chinese mathematicians are particularly intrigued by fuzzy mathematics. The last big conference on fuzzy sets was held in Peking in 1980.

Fuzzy logic is imprecise or fuzzy reasoning with variables that represent fuzzy sets. A fuzzy set is easy to understand. It is simply a set with hazy boundaries; a portion of a continuum along which the parts have no sharp division lines. Put another way, there are elements near the hazy boundary about which one cannot be sure on which side of the fuzzy line they belong.

It is easy to think of common examples: tall and short, young and old, beautiful and ugly, small and large, slow and fast, hot and cold, funny and sad, day and night, living and dead, and so on. Any color word is obviously fuzzy. We constantly reason with such fuzzy truth values as very true, more or less true, probably true, likely false, possibly false, and so on. We constantly use fuzzy quantities such as many, few, some, several, almost all. Even pure mathematicians drift into fuzzy talk about ovals, numbers much larger than 100, a value approximately equal to a specified real number, and so on. The crisp, precise variables of formal logic and mathematics model only a small portion of everyday experience. "There seemed nothing mathematical about the night," Dunsany writes in his novel about computers. "It seemed more like something the owls would understand."

Of course the ancient Greek thinkers were fully aware of the fuzziness of words, and philosophers such as Charles Peirce and John Dewey placed great stress on the fact that, as Peirce once expressed it, all things swim in continua. "Nature," Zadeh likes to say, "writes with a spray can rather than a ballpoint pen." It was not until recently, however, that mathematicians and logicians tried to formalize how human beings actually think with fuzzy concepts.

Mathematicians interested in fuzzy sets have now applied them to just about every mathematical notion you could name. They write papers about fuzzy numbers, algebras, matrices, groups, rings, algorithms, relations, graphs, decisions, probabilities, topologies, limits, and so on. There is something paradoxical about this effort to formalize fuzzy logic because the concept "fuzzy" is itself fuzzy. As Zadeh points out, if a concept is extremely fuzzy it becomes what he calls "vague." Thus "Bob will be back in a few minutes" is a fuzzy statement, but "Bob will be back sometime" is vague. And even though fuzzy set theory and fuzzy logic are precise formal systems, the conclusions of fuzzy logic are fuzzy.

Zadeh is surely right in his belief that shaggy logic underlies both ordinary language and most human thinking. He is convinced that this not only distinguishes human from machine intelligence, but it is what gives human reasoning its superior power. The ability of a grandmaster to play chess, your ability to read poor handwriting, to write a summary of a novel, to play tennis or park a car—such abilities, Zadeh maintains, demonstrate how the ability to manipulate fuzzy concepts is superior to that of any computer program yet devised.

The big question is whether it is possible to formalize a computer language that will model fuzzy reasoning in useful ways. Several such languages are in embryonic stages, including Zadeh's PRUF, an acronym for Possibilistic Relational Universal Fuzzy. Its truth values are linguistic variables, each representing a fuzzy set weighted with a real number in the interval 0 to 1. PRUF is to classical logic, says Zadeh, what the predicate calculus is to the propositional calculus. For a good introduction to fuzzy logic, see Zadeh's "A Theory of Approximate Reasoning" in *Machine Intelligence,* Vol. 9, 1979, and his paper "PRUF—A Meaning Representation for Natural Languages," in the *International Journal of Man-Machine Studies,* Vol. 10, 1978, pp. 395–460.

Is there a useful way, I wonder, to diagram fuzzy logic with fuzzy diagrams?

Real-world logics, which are as formally certain as traditional logic, should not be confused with what is usually called "heuristic reasoning"—informal reasoning by procedures that are not formally perfect but which resemble the intuitive way human minds actually work when confronted by a problem, and which seem to do certain jobs as well as they can be done. Heuristic algorithms are usually developed empirically by studying the ways people think. The best chess programs, for example, have built into them various heuristic rules supplied by grandmasters on the basis of their vast experience. In this area we can put the "analogy reasoning" programs developed by R. E. Kling, John McCarthy's Advice Taker, and the General Problem Solver (GPS) program of Allen Newell and Herbert A. Simon.[2]

How the human mind works remains, of course, a profound mystery. Nerve-nets in the brain have a superficial resemblance to computer networks, and synapses can be looked upon as switching devices. The brain may well be nothing more than an extremely complicated computer made of meat, as Marvin Minsky once put it; but so far no one knows even how memories are recorded, let alone how the brain solves difficult problems, plays master chess, invents a good scientific theory, or creates a memorable tune. Unlike computer circuitry, the brain seems to have evolved so that its thinking involves a great deal of redundancy that protects it from transmission errors. It may make use of processes similar to the error-correcting codes now used for strengthening reliability when sending information over noisy channels. Von Neumann made some valiant efforts to figure out how nerve-nets operate, and the work is continuing, but the truth is that nobody today has any notion of the kind of logic the human brain uses or how it manipulates it. No one even knows how an ant's brain—a wonderfully ingenious miniaturized special-purpose computer—processes its inputs and tells the ant what to do.

A great deal of exciting work is underway on induction programs which examine factual data, experiment with it, and try to find theorems, if the data involves pure logic or mathematics, or laws and theories if the data is drawn from observations of the physical world. A few theorems in logic and mathematics have been discovered by such programs, but efforts to find significant new theorems are still very much in a beginning stage.

The same is true of attempts to write programs that study scientific data and try to come up with good hypotheses. Can the logic of scientific method ever be formalized, perhaps along lines suggested by Rudolf Carnap, by Karl Popper, or by others? If so, computer programs will surely be able to manipulate it. For some recent work in this area, based on Popper's methodology, see "Inductive Inference of Theories from Facts," *Research Report 192* February, 1981, by Ehud Y. Shapiro, a computer scientist at Yale University, and the paper's list of earlier references.[3]

The most ambitious of recent attempts to devise science induction programs has been a series of programs called BACON (after Francis Bacon, one of the earliest philosophers who tried to systematize induction) was initiated in the late seventies by Patrick W. Langley. The latest, BACON 4 (the work of G. L. Bradshaw, Langley, and Simon), will take raw scientific data, search it by heuristic methods, find invariants, and formulate low-level laws.[4]

We should distinguish between finding a law and creating a theory. The demarcating line is not sharp, but in general a theory requires inventing unobservable entities, such as gravitational fields, quarks, and so on, which are then linked in a pattern that will explain a set of laws. The creation of a theory, such as relativity or quantum mechanics, involves creative activity which is dimly understood; at any rate it is far beyond the reach of any present computer program. Inferring a law from empirical data, however, is considerably simpler. It doesn't take much reasoning ability, for instance, if told that metal *a* expands when heated, and metal *b* does likewise, and similarly a hundred other metals, to conjecture that all metals expand when heated.

BACON 4 does much better than that. After being fed the relevant data, it has produced many fundamental laws in physics, such as Kepler's third law of planetary motion, Boyle's law for gases, Snell's law of light refraction, Black's specific heat law, Ohm's electricity law, and a number of other laws of nineteenth-century science, including laws of chemistry, all of which were major discoveries at the time. D. B. Lenat has an induction program for mathematics, called AM, that uses a different method, one closer to theory formation.[5] It searches heuristically for interesting mathematical concepts, then tries to invent good conjectures about them. And there are other induction programs such as meta-DENDRAL.

So far, none has made a discovery not previously known, but who can doubt that they model at least a portion of the kind of thinking in which scientists actually engage? Moreover, there is no good reason why, as these programs improve and better ones are devised, they will not someday discover genuinely new laws, perhaps invent a worthwhile theory or even a new scientific instrument for observing nature.

A closely related problem, on which almost no progress has been made, is that of writing a program that can take a given scientific hypothesis, correlate it with all the relevant observational evidence, and assign a number to the hypothesis that expresses the probability that it will be confirmed (or, as Popper prefers to say, not refuted) by future research. Of course scientists intuitively assign such degrees of confirmation (as Carnap called them) to hypotheses, but they are notoriously fuzzy. A physicist may declare that quantum mechanics has been confirmed to a "very high" degree, but exactly what does this mean? It is all on the same hazy level as statements about heat before thermometers were invented. Everyone was sure fire was hotter than ice, and days were colder in winter than in summer, but when it came to deciding if today is hotter than yesterday, there was room for argument.

I am speaking here of scientific laws and theories, not "factual" conjectures, based on a list of symptoms or a given list of features, such as whether a person has a specified disease or whether a geological formation contains petroleum, copper, uranium, or some other ore. In this narrower domain there are many programs known as "expert systems," such as MYCIN and PROSPECTOR, capable of manipulating "inference nets" and providing excellent estimates of the probability that a certain guess will be confirmed or disconfirmed. Donald Michie has been one of the pioneers in developing such inductive systems, and there is little doubt that they will become more and more useful in many fields of science and technology. But broader conjectures in science present much more formidable difficulties. It may turn out that laws and theories will never submit to crisp quantification, but it would be rash to assume this. If inductive logic ever becomes a workable calculus—even a fuzzy calculus and applicable only in restricted areas of science such as physics—computer programs will certainly be written for reasoning in that calculus. Here again you can keep up with current research on machine logic for inductive reasoning by reading the journals and checking Michie's *Machine Intelligence* volumes.

As computers get smarter and more powerful, and reach the stage where they learn easily and quickly from experience, perhaps design and build other computers, is there a danger they will come "alive" in the sense of acquiring emotions, with human-like hopes and fears, and urges toward self-preservation? Ada Lovelace, Charles Babbage's pretty assistant and intellectual companion, was the first to say that such fears are groundless because calculating machines do only what we tell them to do, or, as phrased today, only what they are wired to do. If a robot does something we don't like, it is frequently remarked, we can just pull the plug.

Charles Peirce, in his article "Logical Machines" (from which we quoted in Chapter 6), argues that, even if a machine could be constructed with the power to "direct itself between different possible procedures" and so thread its way through complicated proofs,

it would still remain true that the machine would be utterly devoid of original initiative, and would only do the special kind of thing it had been calculated to do.[6] This, however, is no defect in a machine; we do not want it to do its own business, but ours. The difficulty with the balloon, for instance, is that it has too much initiative, that it is not mechanical enough. We no more want an original machine, than a housebuilder would want an original journeyman, or an American board of college trustees would hire an original professor.

If Peirce were alive today, perhaps his optimism would be dimmed by the many machines that learn from experience. One of the earliest was W. Gray Walter's *docilis,* a mechanical turtle that acquired conditioned reflexes as it wandered through rooms and bumped into things. Claude Shannon's electronic mouse, which learned how to run mazes, was another simple robot that learned from experience. Arthur Samuel's checkers program was an early game-playing program that steadily improved its skill the more games it played. Michie showed how simple learning machines, for playing games like tick-tack-toe, can actually be constructed out of matchboxes and beads.[7] As computers get better at learning from experience, they soon acquire totally unpredictable behavior patterns. To the degree that they do, they certainly cease to be obedient. They do what they have learned to do, not just what they are wired to do.

How significant is this distinction? It begins to blur when we reflect on the way in which even digital computers learn from experience. After reading an early draft of the last chapter of this book's first edition, William Burkhart said in a letter:

> In doing division a desk calculator subtracts until it gets a negative remainder, adds back until it gets a positive remainder, then shifts and repeats. Similarly, an electronic calculator decides what to do next on the basis of past results of computation. For example, in calculating a table of sines or cosines the machine will guess the first value poorly. But when it computes the next value in the table it will first guess that the answer is the same as the previous answer (a good guess) and go on from that point successively improving its approximations to any desired degree of accuracy. On each successive approximation the machine notes how close its answer is to the previous one. When, finally, two successive answers differ by a negligible amount, the calculator stops approximating and prints its answer.
>
> Is such a machine, which slavishly follows rules, learning? I think not. Rather it is just another machine following rules slavishly. To learn, I believe we must generalize, and this is a creative process. Before building true learning machines we must first learn to build creative and inductive machines. . . .
>
> Machines are things which manipulate symbols exactly as they are wired to do. If we interpret their inputs and outputs as being numbers, then the machine is a computer. If we interpret the answers as logical statements, it is a logic machine. If we connect the outputs to a motor, the machine is a modern elevator control system. If we connect them to a mechanical mouse, it is a parlor game.

In most cases, one's attitude toward these vexing questions will depend on whether one is a philosophical mechanist, regarding man as nothing more than an extremely complicated symbol-manipulating and information-processing machine (doing what it is wired to do by heredity and wired to learn to do from its environment) or an idealist who believes man to be something more than this. To a large extent, this conflict may be a matter of words. William James, for example, believed both in free will and that human personality was capable of surviving death, yet he regarded the human brain as a tool which learns in a manner analogous to the way an earthworm learns. Of course man's powers of learning and thinking are of a much higher order than the powers of an earthworm or Shannon's mechanical mouse, but it is hard to see where a line can be drawn on the evolutionary tree to separate one type of learning from another. There seems to be only a spectrum of increasing neural complexity. As with all spectrums, one can talk about it in words that emphasize continuity and sameness of parts, or in words that emphasize distinctions and differences between the parts.

If the idealist will grant that man's ability to think creatively may arise from an extremely intricate, as yet unknown type of neural structure, the mechanist might be willing to concede that powers of symbol manipulation have emerged from this structure which are qualitatively different from those possessed by man-made machines or even by the lower animals. In the light of these concessions, the two attitudes may not be so far apart as the rhetoric usually employed by both sides would suggest.

Such speculations have little to do with the question of whether robots, in some far-off future, will become cunning enough and disobedient enough to pose a threat to humanity. Is it possible that human thinking will slowly deteriorate over the centuries, as we become more dependent on machine intelligence? Will we some day find ourselves at war with "living" robots who not only do what they have learned to do, but also what they *want* to do, as in so many science fiction tales, including Dunsany's novel?

Rudy Rucker, in Chapter 4 of his *Infinity of the Mind* (Birkhauser Boston, 1982), has a marvelous section of fantasy in which he imagines a possible future for computers if we make the counterfactual assumption that Gödel's incompleteness theorem is not true. Sometime after the year 2000, computers become fast enough and powerful enough to develop a unified formal system in which all mathematical theorems can be proved. The MTM (Mathematical Truth Machine) first cranks out all theorems with one-step proofs, then all with two-step proofs, and so on to a million or more steps. If you can't find the answer to a problem in the computer's memory, just ask the computer and wait a while.

To avoid becoming as obsolete as slide rules, mathematicians begin playing with a "surreal mathematics" based on false axioms, but the MTM wipes out the game by taking a spare hour to produce all the interesting false theorems. As a result of the unification of relativity and quantum theory, physics becomes formalized, and when this system is added to MTM, a PTM (Physical Truth Machine) renders all scientists obsolete.

Aesthetics is next formalized. The ATM (Artistic Truth Machine) creates such satisfying music, paintings, and novels that artists become obsolete. Finally, all human behavior is formalized, and the UTM (Ultimate Truth Machine) makes all thinking obsolete. Computers handle everything, including political decisions, and there is nothing left for people to do except watch sports on the boob tube. Fortunately, Gödel eliminated the possibility of such a depressing

154

scenario by proving that even the MTM, which underlies everything else, is impossible.

There is a strange loophole. Rucker quotes from a 1951 lecture by Gödel[8] a passage stating that there is no reason why a computer might not some day be constructed (Rucker explains how such a computer could evolve) which would be capable of proving all mathematical theorems. However, we could never prove that the computer had this ability, nor could we prove that all its proofs, even in number theory, were in fact valid! We can say the same thing another way. It is conceivable that computers could some day acquire the same intuitive, theorem-proving skills possessed by human minds. They would not operate entirely by general algorithms (we know that is impossible), but by the heuristic thinking methods great mathematicians use.

Jeremy Bernstein, the physicist and writer, recalls that when he was a graduate student he once approached von Neumann to ask him if he believed that computers would ever make mathematicians unnecessary.[9] Von Neumann's reply was "Sonny, don't worry about it."

References

1. "Complexity theory" is the name for the rapidly growing area of computer science concerned with the length of time it takes a computer program to solve a problem. For a good summary of the complexity status of various problems in formal logics, see the section on logic in the appendix of *Computers and Intractability: A Guide to the Theory of NP-Completeness,* by Michael R. Garey and David S. Johnson, W. H. Freeman, 1979.
2. Allen Newell and Herbert Simon, *Human Problem Solving,* Prentice-Hall, 1972.
3. In addition to papers cited by Shapiro, see also "Learning by Being Told and Learning from Examples," by R. S. Michalski and R. L. Chilausky, in which an inductive program is applied to the diagnosis of soybean diseases (*International Journal of Policy Analysis and Information Systems,* Vol. 4, No. 2, 1980, pages 125–161); and "Discovering Rules by Induction from a Large Collection of Examples," by J. R. Quinlan, who applied an inductive program to chess problems (in *Expert Systems in the Micro-Electronic Age,* edited by Donald Michie, Edinburgh University Press, 1979). Similar approaches are being applied to chess by Michie and his group at Edinburgh. See papers in *Advances in Computer Chess 3,* edited by M. R. B. Clarke, Pergamon, 1982.
4. On BACON 4, see Herbert A. Simon, Patrick W. Langley, and Gary L. Bradshaw, "Scientific Discovery as Problem Solving," *Synthese,* Vol. 47, 1981, pp. 1–27. Earlier computer programs were written to find patterns in such induction games as Robert Abbott's card game Eleusis (see my *Scientific American* column, October, 1977) and Sidney Sackson's board game Patterns (see my *Mathematical Circus,* Knopf, 1979, Chapter 4). For programs capable of discovering patterns in

simple sequences of symbols, see Simon's *Models of Thought,* Yale University Press, 1979, Section 5.

5. D. B. Lenat, "Automated Theory Formation in Mathematics," *Proceedings of the Fifth International Joint Conference on Artificial Intelligence,* 1977, pp. 833–842.

6. In L. Frank Baum's *The Road to Oz,* 1909, Tik-tok (a wind-up mechanical man who "thinks, speaks, acts, and does everything but live") is described as being popular with the citizens of Oz for precisely the qualities Peirce finds desirable in a logic machine: "He was so trustworthy, reliable and true; he was sure to do exactly what he was wound up to do, at all times and in all circumstances. Perhaps it is better to be a machine that does its duty than a flesh-and-blood person who will not, for a dead truth is better than a live falsehood."

7. Michie first described his matchbox learning machine, MENACE (Matchbox Educable Noughts and Crosses Engine), in an article on trial and error in *Penguin Science Survey, 1961,* Vol. 2. See also Chapter 8 of my book, *The Unexpected Hanging and Other Mathematical Diversions,* where I apply Michie's idea to a matchbox machine for a simpler board game I called Hexapawn.

8. Gödel's speech has not been published, but Hao Wang reports on it in his book, *From Mathematics to Philosophy,* Humanities Press, 1973.

9. Bernstein, *A Comprehensible World,* Random House, 1967, p. 191.

Appendix

In the first footnote of Chapter 3, I suggested how the shuttle lines of my network diagram could be made "one-way" by using arrows. In the early sixties, Gerrit Mariè Mes, a Dutch-born surgeon at the Medical Center, Krugersdorp, South Africa, who died in 1978, developed a variation of my network method in which "directed graphs" or "digraphs" (as they are now called in graph theory) provided the basis for a logic slide rule and an electrical machine.

Dr. Mes's basic scheme (independently proposed by graph theorist Frank Harary in a conversation I had with him in 1977) is to replace my vertical truth-value lines by two points, one above the other, with the top point (by convention) representing true, the other false. Shuttle lines can now be replaced either by undirected lines (column 2 of Figure 96), directed lines (column 3), or a combination of both (column 4) in which a line without an arrow means that travel may be either way.

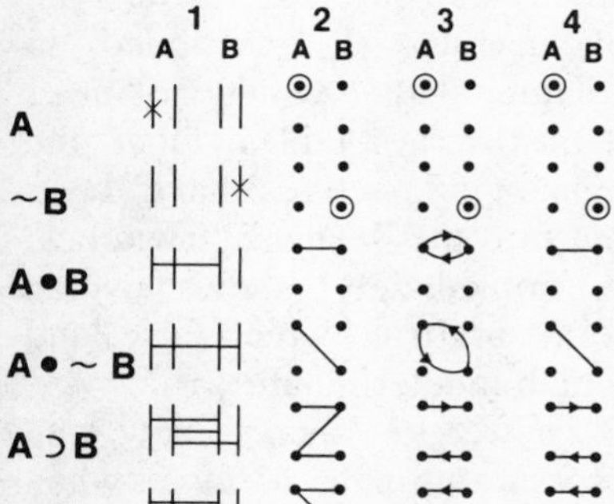

Mes diagramed premises involving these connectives by arranging them on what he called a "deduction strip" along which each relation is separately represented by a four-point digraph, and the connectives join A to B, B to C, C to D, and so on, in a linear or circular fashion. Certain connectives, which Mes called "inverters," change the strip to a Moebius strip. An uneven number of such inverters introduces a contradiction.

By restricting statements to linear or circular form, Mes was able to design an ingenious slide

Figure 96. Logic diagrams of G. M. Mes.

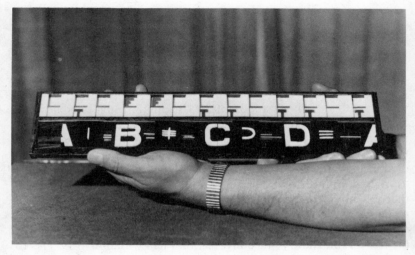

Figure 97. G. M. Mes's logic slide rule.

Figure 98. The logograph of G. M. Mes.

rule for four terms (shown in Figure 97) and an electrical machine for five terms, which he called a "logograph" (Figure 98). It comes close to the type of machine I envisioned in Chapter 8 that would not need to scan truth tables. Once the binary connectives have been put into the device by switches, it immediately shows which terms are true, which false, and which indeterminate.

Figure 99 shows how the problem on page 66 looks when it is diagrammed by an extension of Mes's technique, using the combination of directed and undirected lines.

When all lines are directed, many simple manipulative rules can be stated. For example, to negate a term *n*, switch the two points for *n*, allowing points to

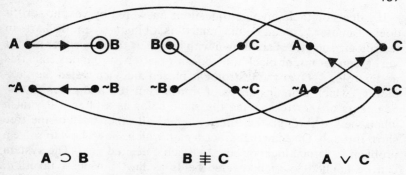

$$A \supset B \qquad B \not\equiv C \qquad A \vee C$$

Figure 99. A diagraph for a problem with three premises.

remain attached to any lines as if the lines were elastic strings. To negate a binary relation, switch each point at the head of an arrow with its companion point. To change a relation to its inverse, simply reverse the direction of all arrows.

As exercises, try using the digraphs for proving De Morgan's laws, for solving the problem on page 67, and exploring ways of handling compound statements, class statements involving "some," and problems in multivalued logics.

Dr. Mes called his logic digraphs "directed iconoglyphs." They are introduced in Chapter 10 and discussed in subsequent chapters of his unpublished book, *Iconic Logic,* now in the possession of his widow. A copy of the manuscript has been placed in the library of Boston College. (Anyone interested in this book can contact Professor Thomas J. Blakeley, Department of Philosophy, Boston College, Chestnut Hill, Massachusetts 02167.)

In 1964, Joseph F. Celko of Atlanta, Georgia, won first place at a National Science Fair in Atlanta for his method of diagraming the propositional calculus and its manipulation by a Chinese abacus, or on a specially designed bead abacus which he called a "slabacus." Celko's diagram, a version of the nested crossmarks technique cited in Note 3 of Chapter 2, was explained by Celko in his unpublished paper "A Matrix Diagram for Symbolic Logic." Questions to Celko can be addressed to Box 11023, Atlanta, Georgia 30310.

In 1977 I was visited by Stavros Foundos, a London accountant, who showed me an ingenious system he had devised which not only applies to the propositional calculus, but is capable of handling a wide range of problems in decision theory logic. Foundos calls his system "testrologic," an acronym for TEsting, SToring and Retrieving Of LOGIC.

160

If a decision table involves questions answered by yes, no, or "it doesn't matter," it can be diagramed as a binary-tree flowchart. In testrologic such trees are drawn with branches that are either red for yes, green for no, or black for "doesn't matter." Foundos calls this a "testrolog." Over the testrolog is placed a device called the "explorer" which contains strips of transparent red and green filters. Segments of the tree having the same color as a filter will vanish when viewed through the filter, whereas all other lines of the tree show through. One can then trace a path which shows how to solve a problem in formal logic or how to reach a desired goal. The system can be applied to such diverse fields as law, business, taxation, medical diagnosis, operations research, game theory—indeed, any field in which goals are reached by binary decisions.

Testrologic was first announced in London's *Financial Times*, June 10, 1980, p. 14. A brief description appeared in the *New Scientist*, July 10, 1980, p. 116. A much more detailed explanation, by Frank George, head of the cybernetics department of Brunel University, Middlesex, was given in a two-part article, "Testrologic," in *Computer Age*, October, 1980, pp. 61–62, and November 1980, pp. 64–65. The system is protected by U.S. patent 4,213,251 (July 22, 1980), and patent applications are pending in Great Britain. A booklet, *Testrologic*, by Foundos, George, and Martin Aylward of the *Financial Times*, was privately published by Foundos in 1980.

Foundos is now devoting much of his time to the teaching of his system and the marketing of testrological devices and materials through his company Decision Tables, Ltd. Anyone interested can write to Mr. Foundos at 6, West Hill, Wembley Park, Middlesex, England.

Rectangular Venn-like diagrams, called "worlds diagrams," for statements both in the propositional calculus and in modal logic, are employed by Raymond Bradley and Norman Swartz in their book *Possible Worlds: An Introduction to Logic and its Philosophy* (Hackett, 1979). The diagrams are used more to make clear the meaning of statements than for problem solving, but applied to modal logic they are useful in testing formulas.

Index